NO
half-truths
ALLOWED

NO half-truths ALLOWED

UNDERSTANDING THE **COMPLETE** GOSPEL MESSAGE

CHRISTINE PAXSON & ROSE SPILLER

Ambassador International
GREENVILLE, SOUTH CAROLINA & BELFAST, NORTHERN IRELAND
www.ambassador-international.com

No Half-Truths Allowed
Understanding the Complete Gospel Message
©2020 by Christine Paxson and Rose Spiller
All rights reserved

ISBN: 978-1-62020-925-7
eISBN: 978-1-62020-940-0

Cover Design and Typesetting by Hannah Nichols
eBook Conversion by Anna Riebe Raats

All rights reserved. No part of this book may be used or reproduced in any manner whatsoever without written permission except in the case of brief quotations embodied in critical articles or reviews.

Unless otherwise indicated, all Scripture quotations taken from The ESV® Bible (The Holy Bible, English Standard Version®). ESV® Text Edition: 2016. Copyright © 2001 by Crossway, a publishing ministry of Good News Publishers. The ESV® text has been reproduced in cooperation with and by permission of Good News Publishers. Unauthorized reproduction of this publication is prohibited. All rights reserved.

Scripture marked NIV taken from THE HOLY BIBLE, NEW INTERNATIONAL VERSION®, NIV® Copyright © 1973, 1978, 1984, 2011 by Biblica, Inc.® Used by permission. All rights reserved worldwide.

Scripture marked AMP taken from The Amplified Bible Copyright © 2015 by The Lockman Foundation, La Habra, CA 90631. All rights reserved.

AMBASSADOR INTERNATIONAL
Emerald House
411 University Ridge, Suite B14
Greenville, SC 29601, USA
www.ambassador-international.com

AMBASSADOR BOOKS
The Mount
2 Woodstock Link
Belfast, BT6 8DD, Northern Ireland, UK
www.ambassadormedia.co.uk

The colophon is a trademark of Ambassador, a Christian publishing company.

We dedicate this, our first book, to our husbands, John Paxson and Ed Spiller. Your love and support mean the world to us. Thank you for sacrificing hours without us so that we could heed God's calling. We couldn't have done this without you! We love you!

ACKNOWLEDGMENTS

We would like to first and foremost thank our Sovereign Lord who has worked in us, through us, and around us to make this book possible! We want to thank our husbands and families who have supported, encouraged, and put up with us! Thank you to our dear friends Kristin Boettner and Linda Borcky for being our biggest cheerleaders! God has truly blessed us with an incredible support system! We would also like to thank all of the ladies who have sat under our Bible Studies. Your enthusiasm and passion for God's Word has been our inspiration! Thank you, too, to Pastor Chris Lenhart for encouraging us to continue in our studies and teaching. Thank you to Gordon-Conwell Theological Seminary and Reformed Theological Seminary for making seminary level online programs and classes available. We would like to thank all of the brilliant theologians, past and present, who have given us fabulous resources and instruction. Last, but not least, thank you to Ambassador International for taking a chance on a couple of unknown authors!

CONTENTS

CHAPTER 1
LAYING THE GROUND WORK 11

CHAPTER 2
GOD THE ALMIGHTY FATHER AND CREATOR 27

CHAPTER 3
DEAD AS A DOOR NAIL 39

CHAPTER 4
BOUND TO SIN THEN FREED TO LIVE RIGHTEOUSLY 49

CHAPTER 5
1 + 1 = 1 57

CHAPTER 6
PROMISES KEPT 65

CHAPTER 7
"AND THE ANSWER IS . . . " 79

CHAPTER 8
THE MULTI-TASKER 91

CHAPTER 9
PRICELESS REWARDS & ROYAL RESPONSIBILITIES 109

CHAPTER 10
COUNTING THE COST 121

CHAPTER 11
NO HALF-TRUTHS ALLOWED 127

HALF-TRUTHS BEING TAUGHT TODAY 135

CONCLUSION 147

BIBLIOGRAPHY 149

Chapter 1

LAYING THE GROUND WORK

If you have ever been to Lancaster County, Pennsylvania, you know that quilting is a big thing. In fact, Lancaster County is known for its numerous shops that sport lovely, handmade quilts created by local Amish women. Quilting has not just been limited to the Amish in Lancaster, though. Many other women (and men) have gotten into this difficult, delicate craft. It seems like almost everywhere you go in Lancaster County, you see these gorgeous, intricate works of art. What if you decided that you wanted to make one of these quilts? You reason that you are fairly handy with a sewing machine, and you know how to cut out shapes. How hard could it be?

You print out a picture of the quilt you want to make, buy some fabric, and dive in. If this is how you were to approach making a quilt for the first time, I can promise you, it would be a disaster! You will shortly come to find that nothing will match up; your measurements will not have taken into account all the seam allowances; and your "quilt" will end up looking like the nearby preschool made it! Creating something this complex and beautiful is not something one can just wing. You need to study the process, equip yourself with the correct tools, and learn from those who are more experienced in quilting than you. And after doing all of the above, you will find that you can create a quilt you can be proud of, but you will also realize that the more you learn, the more there is still to learn!

TAKING STOCK

A person's experience with the Gospel can be a lot like the quilting analogy. The beauty and seemingly simplistic message of the grace and love of God displayed in His only Son dying for us can draw our longing hearts in like moths to a flame; but if we do not take the time to study and understand the full message of the Gospel, we are selling ourselves—and God—short. The Gospel is not just meant to give us the warm fuzzies. It is also not something to wing when witnessing to people. If we do, we could end up with a Gospel message that looks like that preschool quilt! The Gospel is the Word of God and the main message of the entire Bible. It is the saving power of God! Its power is not contained in the eloquence of the messenger, but in the message itself. That is why we need to get it right. Instead of arrogantly thinking, *Of course we know the Gospel—we are Christians*, we need to ask ourselves some questions:

- Do we know and understand the full Gospel message?

- Can we articulate it on a moment's notice?

- Can we adapt our witness to different audiences without changing the message?

- Are we prepared for the questions that will inevitably come when we share the Gospel with someone?

How well does the average person understand the complete Gospel message?

One reporter has asked thousands of college students over the years, "What does it mean to become a Christian?" Ninety percent could not answer the question clearly. He said their answers were all over the place and mixed with different worldly and American ideals.[1]

---

1 Kevin East, "Building Sons Into Men," Crosswalk.com (blog), September 23, 2016, https://www.crosswalk.com/blogs/kevin-east/.

A church website lists the Gospel message as, "The Gospel is the good news that God is restoring our broken lives through the death and resurrection of Jesus Christ."[2]

We were curious how the people around us would answer the question, *How would you explain the Gospel message to someone?* We posed the question to our Facebook friends, inviting them to share their thoughts to help us with our research. We appreciate the honest answers we received! Here are a few:

- "The Gospel is the stunning reality of what Jesus Christ has done for sinners—through His perfect life, His death on the cross, His death defeating resurrection, and His Heavenly ascension—to give us eternal life with Him, out of His undeserved kindness."

- "The Bible is . . . always was . . . and always will be 'The Book of Life.' Most importantly that Jesus came to teach us how to not only survive [and] persevere but to succeed in this life. All to prepare for eternity in Heaven."

- "The ultimate love story that's truth. God sent His only beloved Son Jesus from Heaven to Earth to reflect Himself, and make a way for us through Christ in order to free us, adopt us, and eventually live with Him throughout eternity. The personal relationship with Jesus starts here and now when we say yes to the invitation to be His. Jesus Christ paid the ultimate sacrifice for this relationship!"

You can see from all of the varied answers above, articulating the *actual* Gospel message is no easy task! Something we recently read defines the Gospel as "the incarnation, sinless life, substitutionary death, burial, bodily

---

2   "What's the Gospel?" Calvary Baptist Church.com, accessed October 12, 2018, http://www.calvarybaptistmiddletown.org/cvglobal/?page=gospel&kw=gospel definition biblical&mt=b&loc=9007359&n=g&d=c&adp=2t1&cid=901509073&adgid=47684264289&tid=kwd-305745758046&gclid=CjwKCAjwjIHeBRAnEiwAhYT2h4RMnQVLRWI2s-UM7rl_ZKQfwWNPNeBxHOYT58GUlPJ4wVjKOtrm0ehoCEskQAvD_BwE.

resurrection, ascension and eternal reign of the Son of God, Jesus Christ."[3] While that definition is accurate, there are two major problems. First, it is an incomplete definition. Second, spit that out to a non-believer or new Christian, and you may as well be speaking in Latin!

So important is it to understand the Gospel message, that the ministry "Lies Young Women Believe" gives women fifty questions they should ask a man before falling in love with him. Question number one is "Can you explain the Gospel to me?"[4]

John Calvin said, "Without the gospel everything is useless and vain; without the gospel we are not Christians; without the gospel all riches is poverty, all wisdom folly before God; strength is weakness, and all the justice of man is under the condemnation of God. But by the knowledge of the Gospel, we are made children of God, brothers of Jesus Christ, fellow townsmen with the saints, citizens of the Kingdom of Heaven, heirs of God with Jesus Christ, by whom the poor are made rich, the weak strong, the fools wise, the sinner justified, the desolate comforted, the doubting sure, and slaves free. It is the power of God for the salvation of all those who believe."[5]

For a majority of Christians, clearly answering, "What is the Gospel?" poses a challenge. While they think they know it and understand it, they struggle with verbalizing it. It is important for us to regularly ask ourselves, "What do I believe, and why do I believe it?" It affirms our faith and keeps us alert and discerning when reading and studying all of the "Christian" stuff that is out there. Also, it will help us to articulate clearly and simply to others when witnessing and/or defending our beliefs. At the top of that list of beliefs is certainly the Gospel message.

---

3 Elyse Fitzpatrick, *Because He Loves Me: How Christ Transforms Our Daily Life*, Wheaton, IL: Crossway Books, 2008.
4 Bethany Beal, "50 Questions to Ask Before Falling in Love," Lies Young Women Believe, accessed October 12, 2018, http://www.liesyoungwomenbelieve.com/50-questions-ask-falling-love/?doing_wp_cron=1539359184.3302710056304931640625.
5 Calvin's Commentaries-Complete," Christian Classics Ethereal Library, accessed October 12, 2018, https://www.ccel.org/ccel/calvin/commentaries.i.html.

Let's start with what we know and where we are right now. How would you explain to someone what the Gospel is? On a separate sheet, write down what you would say to a new or non-Christian. This is not meant to be shared. It is just meant for your eyes only, so you can see where you are right now. Then, at the end of the book, we will do this again, so you can compare.

WHERE DO WE GO FOR ANSWERS?

Before we start on what the actual Gospel message is, we need to know where we go to find it! This may seem obvious to most of us, but for others, not so much. One of the five tenants that came out of the Protestant Reformation in the sixteenth century was *Sola Scriptura* (Latin for "only scripture"). Our Reformation fathers believed that Scripture is the only authority on all matters of God, a belief that is clearly reinforced throughout the Bible. One of the most famous Reformers, Martin Luther, believed this principle so deeply, that when he was on trial at the Diet of Worms in 1521, where he was told by the Catholic Church to recant this belief or be killed, he said:

> Unless I am convinced by the testimony of the Scriptures or by clear reason (for I do not trust either in the pope or in councils alone, since it is well known that they have often erred and contradicted themselves), I am bound by the Scriptures I have quoted and my conscience is captive to the Word of God. I cannot and will not retract anything, since it is neither safe nor right to go against conscience . . . May God help me. Amen.[6]

Here are a few of the many verses that reinforce *Sola Scriptura*:

- **Proverbs 30:5-6**: "Every word of God proves true; he is a shield to those who take refuge in him. Do not add to his words, lest he rebuke you and you be found a liar."

---
6 "Martin Luther's Life: The Imperial Diet of Worms," accessed October 12, 2018, https://www.luther.de/en/worms.html.

- **Matthew 4:4**: "But he answered, 'It is written: *Man shall not live on bread alone, but by every word that comes from the mouth of God.*'"

- **Matthew 22:29**: "But Jesus answered them, 'You are wrong, because you know neither the Scriptures nor the power of God.'"

- **2 Timothy 3:15-17**: "And how from childhood you have been acquainted with the sacred writings, which are able to make you wise for salvation through faith in Christ Jesus. All Scripture is breathed out by God and profitable for teaching, for reproof, for correction, and for training in righteousness, that the man of God may be complete, equipped for every good work."

So if Scripture is the *only* authority on all things of God, then it should be obvious that if you want to know where to go to get the full Gospel message, you go to the Bible! Sadly, though, many Christians do not use just the Bible as their only authority on the things of God. They add in other factors like church tradition, their own experiences, and their own feelings.

Going back to the Reformation, one of the reasons that Martin Luther (and all of the other Reformers) were in conflict with the Catholic Church was that while the Reformers saw plainly that Scripture says that the Bible is the only authority on God, the Catholic Church believed it was the Bible, plus church tradition. Church tradition—or "sacred tradition," as it is sometimes called—is that which the church has interpreted, taught, and handed down to subsequent generations as equally authoritative, or sometimes more authoritative, than Scripture.

One example of this is **Matthew 16:18**: "And I tell you, you are Peter, and on this rock I will build my church, and the gates of hell shall not prevail against it." When this verse is put into context with the surrounding verses and with other Scripture, the "rock" Jesus is speaking about is Himself. Although the Greek for Peter is "Petros"—similar to the word *petra*, which means "rock"—throughout Scripture, it is *Jesus* Who is referred to as the Rock.

In Psalm 118:22, the writer is prophesying about the coming Messiah and says, "The stone that the builders rejected has become the cornerstone." He is saying that although the Messiah will be rejected by the builders (a foreshadowing of Jesus' rejection by many of the Jewish people), God's Kingdom and His people (the Church) would be built upon Him. Jesus is saying to Peter, "Go start My Church, which will be built upon Me!"

In the first century, the Catholic Church interpreted this verse to mean that *Peter* was the rock the church would be built on and because of that was given the supreme authority of the Church. He is considered by them to be the first pope. Thus, this is the start of the Papal Dynasty—the church tradition that the pope is the ultimate authority on God, even over Scripture.

The addition of church tradition being just as or more than authoritative than Scripture remains as one of the major divisions between the Protestant and Catholic churches today.

Biblical exegesis is the study of Scripture. Rule number one of biblical exegesis is that Scripture should interpret Scripture. In other words, the way you know you are interpreting a verse of Scripture correctly is that it is able to be backed up by other Scripture. Nowhere else in Scripture is there mention of Peter, or any earthly man, being the supreme authority of the church.

While the previously mentioned verses make it plain that Scripture is the authority on the things of God, they don't mention anything about using church tradition. But be assured, the Bible has a clear message about using church tradition as an authority. **Mark 7:5-9** says:

> And the Pharisees and the scribes asked him, "Why do your disciples not walk according to the tradition of the elders, but eat with defiled hands?" And he said to them, "Well did Isaiah prophesy of you hypocrites, as it is written, 'This people honors me with their lips, but their heart is far from me; in vain do they worship me, teaching as doctrines the commandments of men.' You leave the commandment of God and hold to the tradition of men." And he

said to them, "You have a fine way of rejecting the commandment of God in order to establish your tradition!"

God's Word is crystal clear that we are never to use tradition as a substitute for the truth in Scripture.

As we have said before, Church tradition is not the only thing that gets added to Scripture, and subsequently, added to our Gospel message. Some use their own life experiences and their feelings. In some cases, these even become a substitute for the actual Gospel message. These are the "Follow your heart" Christians. Rather than trust in the God found in the Bible, they trust in a god of their own making. One they see through the lens of their own experiences and emotions. They will even sometimes argue against Scripture, saying, "*My* God would never do that," or "*My* Jesus is going to save everyone!" Their view of God is not one grounded in truth, but in their own ignorance and self-centeredness.

The Bible has some very strong words against using experiences and emotions as our authority:

- **Proverbs 14:12**: "There is a way that seems right to a man, but its end is the way to death."

- **Proverbs 19:2-3**: "Desire without knowledge is not good, and whoever makes haste with his feet misses his way. When a man's folly brings his way to ruin, his heart rages against the Lord."

- **Proverbs 28:26**: "Whoever trusts in his own mind is a fool."

- **Jeremiah 17:9**: "The heart is deceitful above all things, and desperately sick; who can understand it?"

We should note here that church traditions and individual's experiences and feelings are not a bad thing in and of themselves. For example, it is a tradition in many Reformed denominations to "fence" the communion table. This means that prior to passing out the communion elements, the Pastor

LAYING THE GROUND WORK

instructs that the bread and wine (juice) are to be taken only by those who are believers. Non-believers and children who have not yet made a profession of faith are not to partake in the sacrament, but instead, pray that Jesus would reveal Himself to them. There is no exact Scripture that says this is precisely how it should be done, but we can look to **1 Corinthians 11:27-29** to see where this tradition probably originated:

> Whoever, therefore, eats the bread or drinks the cup of the Lord in an unworthy manner will be guilty concerning the body and blood of the Lord. Let a person examine himself, then, and so eat of the bread and drink of the cup. For anyone who eats and drinks without discerning the body eats and drinks judgment on himself.

At the Last Supper, when Jesus first presented bread and wine as a symbol of His body and blood, He set up the first "fence" by saying the sacrament of communion is part of the covenant. This covenant is the New Covenant between God and His elect. Jesus' body and blood (His crucifixion) pay the penalty for their sins and reconciles them to God. All who believe this are part of this covenant, and it is only those belonging to the covenant that should partake in communion. Non-believers who take of the elements of communion are bringing the judgement of God on themselves. Churches that fence the communion table see it as their responsibility to keep that from happening. Going back to the first rule of biblical exegesis, this interpretation/tradition *is* backed up by other Scripture. (See **Matt. 26:28; Mark 14:24; Luke 22:20; John 6:53-58;** and **1 Cor. 10:16-17**.)

Likewise, a person's experiences and feelings can also be a good thing. Our experiences and feelings are part of the makeup of who we are and will certainly be a part of our testimony of what God has done in our lives. However, they are not to replace the Gospel, and they need to be lined up with Scripture to ensure that they are from God. The problem arises when traditions, experiences, and feelings are contradictory to Scripture, yet are considered as valid, or more valid, than the Word of God.

Knowing human tendencies, God makes it clear that tradition is not to be factored in as having the ultimate authority, and trusting in experiences and feelings can be unreliable and sometimes dangerous. Therefore, all three must be lined up with Scripture to ensure they are from God.

And just in case we still need one more reason to make sure the Gospel message we present is the true message from Scripture, Paul says in **Galatians 1:7-9**:

> "There are some who trouble you and want to distort the gospel of Christ. But even if we or an angel from heaven should preach to you a gospel contrary to the one we preached to you, let him be accursed! As we have said before, so now I say again: If anyone is preaching to you a gospel contrary to the one you received, let him be accursed!"

WHERE DO WE FIND THE GOSPEL MESSAGE IN SCRIPTURE?

Now that we have established that the Bible is our only authoritative source, we can begin to search it for the complete Gospel message. Surprisingly, a great place to start is not actually in one of the four Gospels, but in the book of Romans. Paul wrote this epistle to the church in Rome around 57-58 A.D. It is probably the last letter he wrote before he was martyred by beheading. It has been called Paul's *magnus opus* (masterpiece) and is the purest Gospel message in all of the New Testament. In the first four chapters, Paul breaks the Gospel down for us. We will go into each part in detail in the upcoming chapters, but here is an overview:

1. **Romans 1:1-4—The Gospel has been laced throughout all of Scripture since Creation.**

    The gospel of God promised beforehand through his prophets in the holy Scriptures, concerning his Son, who was descended from David according to the flesh, and was declared to be the Son of

God in power according to the Spirit of holiness by his resurrection from the dead, Jesus Christ our Lord.

2. **Romans 1:18-21—All men have sinned against the Almighty God**.

For the wrath of God is being revealed from heaven against all godlessness and unrighteousness of men, who by their unrighteousness suppress the truth. For what can be known about God is plain to them, because God has shown it to them. For his invisible attributes, namely, his eternal power and divine nature, have been clearly perceived, ever since the creation of the world, in the things that have been made. So they are without excuse. For although they knew God, they did not honor him as God or give thanks to him, but they became futile in their thinking, and their foolish hearts were darkened.

3. **Romans 2:1-4; 3:5-8—God's wrath and judgment against us is righteous.**

Therefore you have no excuse, O man, every one of you who judges. For in passing judgment on another you condemn yourself, because you, the judge, practice the very same things. We know that the judgment of God rightly falls on those who practice such things. Do you suppose, O man—you who judge those who practice such things and yet do them yourself—that you will escape the judgment of God? Or do you presume on the riches of his kindness and forbearance and patience, not knowing that God's kindness is meant to lead you to repentance?

But if our unrighteousness serves to show the righteousness of God, what shall we say? That God is unrighteous to inflict on us? (I speak in a human way.) By no means! For then how could God judge the world? For if through my lie God's truth abounds to his glory, why am I still being condemned as a sinner? And why not do evil that good may come?—as some people slanderously charge us with saying. Their condemnation is just!

4. **Romans 3:22-24, 28; 4:13-17—We are saved from God's wrath, not by anything we can do, but only by having faith in the saving work of Jesus Christ.**

   The righteousness of God through faith in Jesus Christ for all who believe. For there is no distinction: for all have sinned and fall short of the glory of God, and are justified by his grace as a gift through the redemption that is in Christ Jesus . . . For we hold that one is justified by faith apart from the works of the law.

   For the promise to Abraham and his offspring that he would be heir of the world, did not come through the law but through the righteousness of faith. For if it is the adherents of the law who are to be the heirs, faith is null and the promise is void. For the law brings wrath, but where there is no law there is no transgression. That is why it depends on faith, in order that the promise may rest on grace and be guaranteed to all his offspring—not only to the adherent of the law, but also to the one who shares in the faith of Abraham, who is the father of us all. As it is written: "I have made you a father of many nations"—in the presence of the God in whom he believed, who gives life to the dead and calls into existence the things that do not exist.

Romans can be summarized this way: **God Creates—Man Sins—Christ Redeems—Man Responds.**

UNDERSTANDING OUR WITNESS

Too often, we hear Christians witness the Gospel by saying cliché lines like, "God loves you," or "Trust in Jesus." We need to understand that this is not the Gospel. It is a half-truth. Not only is it too simplistic, but it is giving your listener an inaccurate and less-than-full picture of what God's Word says. As Albert Einstein said, "Everything should be made as simple as possible, but no simpler."[7]

---

[7] "Albert Einstein - Everything Should Be Made as Simple as Possible, but No Simpler," Championing Science, accessed October 12, 2018, https://championingscience.com/2013/11/10/everything-should-be-made-as-simple-as-possible-but-no-simpler/.

Following Einstein's thinking, before we can know how simple or not simple to make our Gospel presentation, we need to know our audience. Once again, we can go to Paul for a model for this. Paul was a master at knowing his audience and tailoring his witness to them. The message never changed, but the language he used did. When Paul was teaching the Greeks in Athens, he used the idols they had made to their pagan gods as a stepping stone for teaching them about Jesus. When he spoke to the Jewish people, he didn't need to elaborate on how bad their sin condition was because they already understood from the Old Testament that they had an inherent sin nature.

In contrast, the Gentile church in Corinth did not know the Old Testament and did not understand inborn sin. They were becoming mired in sin by false teaching and syncretism and needed a strong rebuke from Paul about it. We need to understand our listeners as Paul did. We need to know what kind of background they are coming from, their current understanding of Scripture and Christianity, and their openness to God. Our message should *never* change; but our delivery, depending on who we are speaking to, may.

Through the years, evangelists have come up with some different methods of witnessing: Evangelism Explosion, the Romans Road, or Four Spiritual Laws, to name a few. These were blanket methods used for everyone. Sometimes, they were successful, and sometimes they weren't. As Paul shows us, we need to adopt a more tailor-made method, rather than a one-size-fits-all. A recent article from the Gospel Coalition gives us a good springboard to use today:

> In a secularized society, core Christian beliefs can't be assumed. We must still preach justification by faith through the death and resurrection of Christ, but we may start in Genesis rather than Romans. Increasingly, the people to whom we are delivering the gospel will not be former Roman Catholic altar boys or lapsed Lutherans, but people for whom the entire Christian story is foreign. Before we tell them what Paul says about their sin, we may need to tell them what sin is and why Paul matters.

In some ways this change is freeing. It allows us to do what we should have been doing all along: retelling the entire Bible's whole story, from creation to fall to redemption to consummation. In a sense, a whole-Bible, one-story gospel releases us from the temptation to close the deal and produce fake conversions or offer a kind of fire insurance that doesn't truly save. Secularists aren't interested in insurance from a fire that they don't believe in.[8]

Think about those in your life to whom you would like to witness the Gospel. What different tactics might you need for each of them? Do they have any understanding of the Bible, or do you need to go back to Genesis to begin your witness?

WHY WITNESS THE GOSPEL

I have heard people say that since the Holy Spirit is the One Who regenerates people's hearts and moves them toward God, why is it necessary that we evangelize to people? Their reasoning is that if God saves those He elects, they will be saved whether we witness to them or not. There are two reasons why sharing the Gospel with people is essential. First, because God says it is! **Mark 16:15** says, "And he (Jesus) said to them, 'Go into all the world and proclaim the gospel to the whole creation.'" That alone should be reason enough for any Christian!

However, if you need a second reason, here it is. Although God doesn't need us to save anybody, He gives us the privilege of being part of the process. We have no idea whose heart the Holy Spirit may be working in, and it is not our place to try and figure it out. We are to assume everyone is either saved or not yet saved. We are to witness to everyone and let God do the rest. And even though we aren't the ones doing the saving, being a part of someone coming

---

8   Daniel Darling, "3 Ways Rising Secularism Affects Evangelism," *The Gospel Coalition*, accessed October 12, 2018, https://www.thegospelcoalition.org/article/3-ways-rising-secularism-affects-evangelism/.

to saving faith in Jesus Christ is one of the most rewarding and humbling things that will ever happen to you! Therefore, it is crucial that we present the accurate Gospel to them. Presenting less does damage to our witness and is not honoring to God. The only stumbling block a person should have when they come to Christ is Jesus Himself, not something we are adding or taking away from the Gospel message.

Now, let's begin looking at the distinct parts of the Gospel!

Chapter 2

GOD THE ALMIGHTY FATHER AND CREATOR

We summed up the Gospel as Paul records it in the book of Romans as *God creates; man sins; Christ redeems; and man responds.* Before we can flesh out the "God creates" part of the Gospel, we need to first get a foundational understanding of Who God is.

GOD THE FATHER AS PART OF THE TRINITY

At God's very foundation is the Trinity. While nowhere in the Bible is the term "Trinity" used or fully explained, our early church fathers carefully examined all of Scripture to generate the doctrine of the Trinity. The doctrine of the Trinity has three major truths:

(1) The Father, Son, and Holy Spirit are distinct Persons;

(2) Each Person is fully God; and

(3) There is only one God.

Stated another way, there is one God Who eternally exists as three Persons (for lack of a better word): God the Father, Jesus the Son, and the Holy Spirit. God is one in essence and three in person. All three are God—all equal, all omnipotent (all-powerful), all omniscient (all-knowing), and all omnipresent (present everywhere). This doctrine is crucial to our Christian faith and is essential for properly understanding God as the Father, the Son, and the Holy Spirit.

While all Three are one God, They are all distinct. And while They are all the same in nature and all have the same attributes, They do have different functions. It is important to understand Their functions. **First Peter 1:1-2** gives us a quick glimpse at each of Their purposes: "To those who are elect exiles of the Dispersion in Pontus, Galatia, Cappadocia, Asia, and Bithynia, according to the foreknowledge of God the Father, in the sanctification of the Spirit, for obedience to Jesus Christ and for sprinkling with his blood."

This verse (along with others) summarizes the roles played by each of the three Persons of the Trinity as:

Father—Creator, Elector

Jesus—Savior, King, Intercessor

Holy Spirit—Regenerator, Counselor, Sanctifier

When we understand the Trinity, we understand that the Trinity is not just three different ways of looking at God, nor is it different roles God plays at different times. The Father is never the Son; the Son is never the Holy Spirit; and the Holy Spirit is never the Father. All Three are one God, yet three distinct Persons; and All have existed for all time simultaneously. Any attribute Scripture ascribes to one of the Persons of the Trinity can also be ascribed to the Other Two.

Second Corinthians 13:14 gives us a beautiful picture of the Trinity: "The grace of the Lord Jesus Christ and the love of God and the fellowship of the Holy Spirit be with you all." The love of God the Father prompts Him to choose a people to reconcile to Himself. He does this first, through the grace of Jesus, manifested by Jesus' going to the cross as the ransom for God's people, and then by indwelling believers with the Holy Spirit to fellowship and sanctify us. It is with God the Almighty Father and Creator that we begin the Gospel.

GOD THE ALMIGHTY HOLY FATHER

Jesus refers to God the Father as "Holy Father" in John 17:11. Further, when Jesus instructs His disciples on how to pray in Matthew 6:9-13, He begins in verse 9 with "Our Father in heaven, hallowed be your name." The definition of *hallowed* is "holy." This corresponds with John 17:11 and other verses in the Bible, where God is referred to as holy. All are saying the same thing. The definition of *holy* is "exalted or worthy of complete devotion as one perfect in goodness and righteousness; consecrated; sacred."[9] Being consecrated and sacred means that God is separate from us, and there is no one who is on the same level as He is.

The Catholic Church uses the title "holy father" for the Pope. Looking at the definition of holy, we challenge this. Is there a human being (other than Jesus) who has ever lived that could possibly deserve this title? Nobody, except God, should be called Holy Father. We are not alone in this thinking. Back in 2014, Rick Warren, pastor of Saddleback Church in California, was heavily criticized and called blasphemous by many evangelicals for addressing Pope Francis as the holy father.[10]

How holy is God the Father? **Isaiah 6:3** says, "Holy, holy, holy is the Lord of hosts; the whole earth is full of his glory!" The late, brilliant R.C. Sproul offers a great insight into this verse: "The Bible says that God is holy, holy, holy. Not that He is merely holy, or even holy, holy. He is holy, holy, holy. The Bible never says that God is love, love, love, or mercy, mercy, mercy, or wrath, wrath, wrath, or justice, justice, justice. It does say that He is holy, holy, holy, the whole earth is full of His glory."[11]

When we describe God, we often do it by listing His attributes. We may say God is love; God knows everything; God is a Spirit; God is just; God is

---

9 *Merriam-Webster*, s.v. "holy," accessed December 12, 2018, https://www.merriam-webster.com/dictionary/holy.
10 "Rick Warren Calls Pope 'Holy Father,'" Pulpit & Pen.com, accessed October 12, 2018, https://pulpitandpen.org/2014/11/18/rick-warren-calls-pope-holy-father/.
11 R.C. Sproul, *The Holiness of God*, Carol Stream, IL: Tyndale House Publishers, 2006.

merciful; and so on. Our tendency is to add *holy* to this list. Holy becomes just one more characteristic of God. But when the word *holy* is applied to God, it does not mean one, single attribute. God's holiness is not just one quality among many. It permeates everything He is and everything He does. God's love is holy love. God's justice is holy justice; God's knowledge is holy knowledge; God's Spirit is the Holy Spirit, etc.

When we understand that the holiness of God seeps into everything about Him, it can make us see Him in a whole new light. Let's look at some verses that describe attributes of God with, perhaps, a fresh outlook, understanding now that these attributes are holy.

- **Exodus 20:5**—"For I the Lord your God am a jealous God." Jealousy usually has negative connotations—probably because while the feeling of jealousy is not a sin, it is almost always acted out sinfully. But God's jealousy is a holy jealousy. His jealousy means that He is "earnestly protective and watchful" of His honor as He is worthy of complete devotion.

- **Exodus 34:6-7**—"The Lord, the Lord, a God merciful and gracious, slow to anger, abounding in steadfast love and faithfulness." As beautiful and comforting as this verse is, how much more so when we know that God's compassion, grace, patience, love, and faithfulness are holy! They are far and above any human manifestations of these feelings!

- **Numbers 23:19**—"God is not man, that he should lie, or a son of man, that he should change his mind." God is all-knowing, all-powerful, and sovereign over everything. It's not just that He doesn't lie or change His mind; it's that it isn't even a possibility for Him to do so. If He knows all—past, present, and future—and that knowledge is perfect, everything He says and does is always truthful and will come to pass. Since He has sovereignly planned out all of time since before He created the world, He has no reason to change His mind.

- **Deuteronomy 4:31**—"For the LORD your God is a merciful God. He will not leave you or destroy you or forget the covenant with your fathers that he swore to them." Because God is holy and perfect in goodness, we can stand on this promise, and all of His promises, with complete assurance that what He pledges will always come to be, no matter what.

- **Deuteronomy 32:4**—"The Rock, his work is perfect, for all his ways are justice." This verse is pretty self-explanatory, but His works and ways are not just perfect and just, but holy perfect and holy just, meaning perfect in righteousness!

- **Psalm 46:1**—"God is our refuge and strength, a very present help in trouble." A favorite verse of many for good reason. God is our holy Refuge, our holy Strength, and our holy, ever-present Help.

- **Habakkuk 1:13**—"You who are of purer eyes than to see evil and cannot look at wrong." Because God is holy and sacred, He is unable to look on evil. Because His love is a perfect, holy love, He is unable to let wrongs go unpunished.

- **1 Corinthians 14:33**—"For God is not a God of confusion but of peace." God creates and sustains creation with a holy order. There is nothing chaotic or random in anything He does.

- **James 1:13**—"God cannot be tempted with evil, and he himself tempts no one." Because God is holy, not only is He not tempted by evil, but He is also unable to tempt anyone. To do that would be sinful, and He is incapable of sinning.

- **1 John 4:16**—"God is love." God's love is a holy, perfect love. This is not the warm, fuzzy, emotional feeling that we may think about love.

THE NAMES OF GOD

If you want to gain a good understanding of Who God is, just look at His names. We could probably write an entire book just on the Hebrew names for God used throughout the Old Testament and another volume on His names in the New Testament. Let's just look at a few.

- **Yahweh**—The name Yahweh was a personal, sacred name for God, meaning "I am." So sacred was it, that it was never spoken out loud. When it was written down, the vowels were left out just to be sure it wasn't being used irreverently. It would have been recorded as YHWH. Yahweh is the most used name for God in the Old Testament. (Sometimes "Adonai" is used, but that was a replacement word for the sacred name of Yahweh.) When you read your Old Testament and see "LORD" in all caps, that is where Yahweh was used in the original Arameic/Hebrew. Jehovah is the English translation of YHWH.

- **El Shaddai**—El Shaddai means "God Almighty." This term was mostly used in the patriarchal narratives in Genesis and in the poetic books of the Bible.

- **Elohim**—Elohim means "infinite, all-powerful God." It is the name for God used in Genesis 1:1 (emphasis mine)—"In the beginning <u>God</u> (Elohim) created the heavens and the earth."

- **El Elyon**—El Elyon means "God most high." An example of where it is used is Psalm 57:2 (emphasis mine): "I cry out to <u>God Most High</u> (El Elyon)."[12]

The biblical authors understood what we should all understand by now—God is perfect and so much higher than us that He is beyond our full

---

12 "O.T. Names of God—Study Resources," Blue Letter Bible, accessed October 18, 2018, https://www.blueletterbible.org/study/misc/name_god.cfm.

comprehension. He is deserving of our praise, worship, and complete devotion. He is holy!

GOD, THE ALMIGHTY CREATOR

Now that we have a foundational understanding of God, let's begin to look at the first part of the Gospel—God creates. The best place to start is to start at the beginning: **Genesis 1:1**—"God created the heavens and the earth." This is the very essence of Who God the Father is. He is the Creator. If we get this wrong, everything that follows will be wrong.

Isaiah 55:12-13 tells us that creation sings the praises of God the Creator. God created the world, and He created us. This is enormous! When making a quilt, one needs to begin at the end. You start with a finished pattern, then work backwards by choosing fabric and cutting it to the exact shape and measurements, piecing it, and finally, sewing it all together. Throughout the different stages, it may look like a jumbled mess, but there is a definitive plan to what you are doing. Before God ever created one molecule of this world, He already knew what His finished plan would be. Having that finished plan, He then created the world and us to be a part of that plan. From Creation up until the completion of the plan—when Jesus comes back—you can say that we are in the construction phase of that plan.

When making a quilt, you wouldn't include fabric or thread that you don't need for completion of your project. God doesn't either! Everyone and everything throughout history, since the creation of the world, has been part of God's plan. This means everyone has purpose. Even when God has wiped out entire civilizations, it has been for His plan. So while some of these accounts in the Bible may be difficult for us to read, we can find some comfort in the fact that even the people whom God destroyed had purpose.

During the working stage of making a quilt, it can look like a jumbled-up mess to everyone but the quiltmaker. Only the creator understands where everything is going and how it will all work together in the end. It can sometimes be that way with God and what is going on in the world. But rest assured, God knows exactly how everything will come together. There are no "oops" with God. God is, and has always been, all-knowing, all-powerful, and completely sovereign over everything! *Everyone* has been created for a purpose and has a place in God's plan. This fact gives our lives meaning! While the ultimate purpose of all men is to glorify God and enjoy Him forever, God has created each of us with a specific, tailor-made purpose that is just for us.

Knowing we have purpose should give us confidence; but it also presents us with great responsibility. While we can never be outside of God's decretive will, we can disobey His preceptive or revealed will. To put it simply, God has sovereignly ordained things that will *always* come to pass, regardless of what we do or don't do. This is God's decretive will.

We have no way of knowing what that decretive will is, nor should we try and figure it out. However, God has laid out what He expects of us in His precepts and commands in the Bible. This is God's preceptive will. It is this will that we are privy to and this will that we sin against. Our responsibility is to study Scripture to learn the preceptive will of God and strive to be obedient to it. This is part of the sanctification (spiritual maturation) process. And while the Holy Spirit is sovereign over our sanctification, we participate by cooperating with Him. We are called to know and submit to the laws and commands of God. Obviously, we won't ever perfect this during our lifetime. This doesn't even necessarily mean that we will sin less; but it does mean that we will become more and more aware of our sin and will turn to God in repentance sooner.

When we understand that God is our Creator, it not only brings our lives purpose and gives us responsibility, but it also helps us understand that no one is autonomous. This is key to the Gospel! Since we are created by God, we are owned by God; and He has the right to tell us how He wants us to live. Let's look at this passage from **Job 38:1-11**:

Then the LORD answered Job out of the whirlwind and said: **2** "Who is this that darkens counsel by words without knowledge? **3** Dress for action like a man; I will question you, and you make it known to me. **4** "Where were you when I laid the foundation of the earth? Tell me, if you have understanding. **5** Who determined its measurements—surely you know! Or who stretched the line upon it? **6** On what were its bases sunk, or who laid its cornerstone, **7** when the morning stars sang together and all the sons of God shouted for joy? **8** "Or who shut in the sea with doors when it burst forth from the womb, **9** when I made clouds its garment and thick darkness its swaddling band, **10** and prescribed limits for it and set its bars and doors, **11** and said, 'Thus far shall you come, and no farther, and here shall your proud waves be stayed'?"

God goes on like this with Job for quite some time, but you get the picture. Prior to these verses, Job, who has had countless tragedies befall him, is questioning why God is allowing all of these things to happen to him. These verses in chapter thirty-eight are part of God's response to Job. God is putting Job (and through Job, us) in his place. The bottom line is God created the world, and He created us. He knows all; we know nothing. Yet even though God has every right to tell us how to live, He does not just give us arbitrary rules and regulations to be a killjoy. He gives us laws and commands that are best for us and that will make life go better for us. God is good! He knows *and* wants what is best for us!

In a nutshell, *sin* is man's rejection of God's laws and commands, and thus, man's rejection of God, Himself. As we will see, the Gospel is God's response to that rejection.

JUSTICE BRINGS FORTH PUNISHMENT

We said earlier, everything about God is holy. This means His justice is also holy. What does holy and perfect justice look like? The answer is obvious—that everyone gets what they deserve. People seem to have no issue in accepting that God shows love and mercy, but they struggle with the fact that God punishes sin. After all, punishing is not very loving. How could a God Who is perfect Love send someone to Hell just for doing some bad things? In our next chapter, we will talk about those "bad things"; but for now, yes, while it is true that God is perfect Love, His love does not cancel out His justice and righteousness.

In fact, how perfect would Love be if it overlooked sin and injustice? If God ignored sin, it would make Him inconsistent, untrustworthy, immoral, and worst of all, weak. Would you really want to worship a God like that? Of course not! We want a God Who is strong, moral, just, trustworthy, and never-changing. Even people who insist they don't want a God Who judges and punishes don't fully mean it. Think of Nero, Hitler, Stalin, Osama Bin Laden, and Kim Jong-un, to name just a few. Who doesn't want to be assured that even though it appears these men got away with untold amounts of evil while here on Earth, someday they will have to answer to a just God? And unless they have come to a saving grace in Jesus, they will be punished as their crimes deserve.

When people say they don't want a God Who is judgmental, what they really mean is that they don't want God to judge them! "Punish the 'real' bad guys, Lord, but look the other way when we 'good' guys slip up." Kind of like if you get stopped for speeding and tell the police officer to spend his time going after the real criminals.

Just as good cannot exist without evil, happiness cannot exist without sadness, and joy cannot exist without pain, neither can the saving work of Jesus exist without the punishment we need saving from! Only when we understand the holiness of God the Almighty Creator and Father can we understand the seriousness and evil of our sin against that holy God. That comprehension makes the saving work of Jesus all the sweeter! For what can be a sweeter message to someone who has been deservedly condemned to die for their crime than that they have not only received a stay of execution, but have received a full pardon! Friends, if you belong to Jesus, He has done this for you for every sin you have committed, every sin you will commit, and even for every sin you will never be aware that you committed! Jesus has permanently reconciled us to our Almighty Father Who now looks on us as His beloved children!

Having a healthy reverence for God and His holiness is the biblical definition of the "fear of the Lord." Proverbs 9:10 says, "The fear of the Lord is the beginning of wisdom." To truly comprehend what it means to have a healthy reverence for God, we need to take a serious look at our sin. We need to understand exactly what it is we have done to offend God's holiness.

Chapter 3

DEAD AS A DOOR NAIL

At the end of the last chapter, we talked about the holiness of God and the saving work of Jesus that rescues us from the punishment from which we need to be saved. But when you hear those words, do you really believe that you need rescuing from God's punishment?

When you think of God, how do you picture Him in your mind? What do you think He's like? And what do you think He thinks about you? What's He thinking when you do something "good"? More importantly, what is He thinking when you do something "bad"? What, exactly, are your thoughts about how God views sin? And what is sin, really? Certainly, that can't mean your "little mistakes" or "slip-ups" that happen on a regular basis, can it? Let's be honest—you might have gossiped about your neighbor this morning and yelled at your kids (and the cat) all before breakfast, but you're not as bad as a lot of people in the world—you're not an axe murderer or anything!

And what went wrong in the first place? Why do people do bad things? We're all born innocent, aren't we? Who taught us to do bad things? Who taught us to sin? Does the devil make us do it? Is he sitting on one shoulder, with God (or an angel) on the other—both trying to coax us to make the choice that suits their side? And why does any of it matter, since most of us are pretty good people? In the end, for most of us, the good and bad we do probably all equals out in God's eyes, doesn't it?

Most of us have had these basic, fundamental questions—and others like them—run through our heads at one time or another. For some of us, the Bible has been taught in a way that makes us believe many of these things are right. For others, culture, other religions' ideas, and even TV commercials have planted these ideas firmly in our minds. But we need to know what the Bible says about them. Remember, the goal for this book is to make sure that by the end, you have a clear understanding of what the full Gospel message is—not only for yourself, but also so that when you share it with others, they fully understand what they are either accepting or rejecting.

The Gospel is presented in so many different ways today, many of which have nothing at all to do with sin. To present it as less than what it is can leave people with a false sense that they are saved, a hope that if they became a Christian all of the bad things in their lives would get better, false ideas about God, or an incorrect view of what living the Christian life really means.

To find what the Bible has to say about God, the human condition, and sin, we must go back to the start, back to the beginning of life here on Earth. The answer started earlier than that, really, but we'll get to that later. To begin, let's look at why God created us in the first place.

WHY DID GOD CREATE US?

One of the most fundamental questions all humans have is "What is my purpose?" The first question in the Westminster Shorter Catechism (WSC) gives us the answer from the Bible. The WSC puts it this way: "What is the chief end of man?" And the answer is: "Man's chief end is to glorify God and enjoy him forever."[13] Humans were created to glorify and worship God in all that we do, and in doing so, to find ultimate enjoyment in Him. We see Paul and David (among others) tell us these truths: "Let them praise the name

---

13   Douglas F. Kelly, Philip B. Rollinson, and Frederick T. Marsh, *The Westminster Shorter Catechism in Modern English*, Phillipsburg, NJ: Presbyterian and Reformed Pub., 1986.

of the LORD! For he commanded and they were created" (**Psalm 148:5**). "So, whether you eat or drink, or whatever you do, do all to the glory of God" (**1 Cor. 10:31**). "Whom have I in heaven but you? And there is nothing on earth that I desire besides you" (**Psalm 73:25**).

We see this again in Isaiah, with God assuring Israel that He will deliver and restore them because they are His people, who were created by Him, who are called by His name, and who were created for His glory. Take in the meaning of these words from **Isaiah 43:1-7**:

> But now thus says the LORD, he who created you, O Jacob, he who formed you, O Israel: "Fear not, for I have redeemed you; I have called you by name, you are mine. When you pass through the waters, I will be with you; and through the rivers, they shall not overwhelm you; when you walk through fire you shall not be burned, and the flame shall not consume you. For I am the LORD your God, the Holy One of Israel, your Savior. I give Egypt as your ransom, Cush and Seba in exchange for you. Because you are precious in my eyes, and honored, and I love you, I give men in return for you, peoples in exchange for your life. Fear not, for I am with you; I will bring your offspring from the east, and from the west I will gather you. I will say to the north, Give up, and to the south, Do not withhold; bring my sons from afar and my daughters from the end of the earth, everyone who is called by my name, whom I created for my glory, whom I formed and made."

God really did create us for His glory! And He is God; He will be glorified. No one can stop Him from it!

Does knowing why God created you make you re-think your purpose here on Earth? Does it make you realize what the overarching, central theme of your life should be and what you should do with each day that you're given? If you are a Christian, you are loved, protected, and ransomed by the One Who created you!

But you may be wondering, if God loves us so much and wants us to glorify Him, what happened to the world He created? Terrorist attacks, robberies, animal cruelty all make the headlines, sadly, on a regular basis. Reports about such things are so prevalent in the world, that even stories of the worst of it sometimes barely catch our attention. Satan wants sin to seem normal. The more normal it seems (the more we see others doing it), the less it seems like sin! But where did all this start?

A FALL IN THE GARDEN

Humans who say they don't believe in God can't come up with an answer to why there's so much bad in the world. In fact, in trying to answer, they can get themselves into quite a conundrum. For them, there is no good starting place to find where people go wrong. But as Christians, we look to the Bible for answers, and in doing so, we find exactly what went wrong.

After God created Adam and Eve, He blessed them and gave them these instructions: "Be fruitful and multiply and fill the earth and subdue it, and have dominion over the fish of the sea and over the birds of the heavens and over every living thing that moves on the earth" (**Gen. 1:28**). Adam and Eve were given dominion over every other creature on the earth. This dominion was not complete either. They were not free to do whatever they pleased with God's creation. They were always to remember that they were under God's authority. As their Creator, He is the One Who gave them any authority they had. They were dependent on Him, even for their very lives.

The tree of the knowledge of good and evil was a reminder of that fact. In **Genesis 2:17**, God tells them about this tree. This tree comes with a blessing and curse—don't eat of it, and you will live; eat of it, and you will die. No one was going hungry here; Adam and Eve had been given the right to eat from every seed-yielding plant and tree whose fruit yielded seed, and the animals had been given every green plant for food (yes, they were all vegetarians!). But the tree of the knowledge of good and evil was off-limits for one simple reason . . . because God said so.

Some of us probably remember a time when an elementary school principal was allowed to use a wooden paddle on the backside of any student who broke the rules. Even if you never had this happen to you personally, the sound of the paddle and cries of the student that echoed down the hall were definitely a deterrent. The paddle hung in the school office in plain sight. It was a reminder that there would be consequences for breaking the rules. We could not make our own rules—someone else was the authority in the school. Adam and Eve could not make their own rules either. God was in charge. As Creator, He has the right to make all the rules. Eating from the tree of the knowledge of good and evil came with consequences—death.

Adam and Eve were created in God's image, just as all humans are. Therefore, we say all human life has value and worth. However, there is one difference between our first parents and the rest of us: Adam and Eve had the ability to not sin. This is an ability no other human being has had—except for Jesus Incarnate—ever since they ate from the forbidden tree.

Because they had the ability to live life in a totally righteous and pleasing manner to God, fully obeying Him, Adam and Eve lived under what we call the covenant of works: as long as they obeyed God and lived subject to what He told them, things would be good for them, and they would enjoy unbroken fellowship with God forever. The Westminster Confession of Faith puts it this way:

> After God had made all other creatures, He created man, male and female, with reasonable and immortal souls, endued with knowledge, righteousness, and true holiness, after His own image; having the law of God written in their hearts, and power to fulfill it; and yet under a possibility of transgressing, being left to the liberty of their own will, which was subject unto change. Beside this law written in their hearts, they received a command, not to eat of the tree of the knowledge of good and evil; which while they kept, they were happy in their communion with God, and had dominion over the creatures.[14]

---

14 Ibid.

However, Adam and Eve decided to disobey God and eat the fruit from the tree of the knowledge of good and evil. They decided to sin. We see this in Genesis 3:1-7. This sin of theirs is what we commonly refer to as "the fall of man." Adam and Eve did not just "eat some forbidden fruit." By eating, they were making a conscious declaration that they did not want to be subject to anyone else's authority to determine what was good and what was evil; they wanted to decide for themselves what was good and what was not. They were rejecting their Creator in some vain attempt to be like Him. And they threw caution to the wind in regard to the consequences of which they'd been told.

S-I-N

Sin is not the "isolated bad things we do," and it is definitely not "mistakes" or "mess-ups," as it is commonly referred to today. Sin is an offense against our Creator God and, therefore, justly deserves punishment. Remember how we talked about not just wanting a loving God, but also a righteous and just God? One who would not overlook the atrocities and injustices in our world? One who would not overlook bad things done to you (and me) by others? Well, that is exactly what we have! BUT, if the thought of God bringing justice to your enemies made you just stand up and cheer or wish that you could insert the clapping emoji here, you'd better sit down! This should be a sobering thought because what could deserve punishment more than disobeying the One Who made and sustains the universe; the One who created Adam and Eve, and you, and me? And just like Adam and Eve and our enemies, we (you and me) sin every day. We carry out injustices against our Creator every day.

God had told our first parents that if they ate the fruit of that tree, they would die. But as we know, it was not an instantaneous death. Part of the curse was that Adam and Eve were banished from the garden; their work would be toilsome; there would be pain in childbirth; they would feel guilt and condemnation. And worst of all, they became alienated from God. They weren't just separated from Him; they actually became objects of His wrath, as we're told in Ephesians 2:1-3:

> And you were dead in the trespasses and sins in which you once walked, following the course of this world, following the prince of the power of the air [Satan], the spirit that is now at work in the sons of disobedience—among whom we all once lived in the passions of our flesh, carrying out the desires of the body and the mind, and were by nature children of wrath, like the rest of mankind.

Paul expounds on our being objects of God's wrath in Romans 1:18-32, a passage used often to point out sexual sin, but a passage that, in reality, deals with many kinds of sin—ones that we are all guilty of routinely. The point is, our sin has made us objects of God's wrath.

What does Adam and Eve's sin have to do with us? The consequences of Adam and Eve's sin did not end with them. Adam and Eve brought death and other curses into the world that affected all of creation. Adam is linked with the patriarchs, and through them, to the rest of humanity by natural genealogy (to Noah, Abraham, Isaac, and Jacob in Genesis chapters five, ten, and eleven).

Adam's sin tainted every person's nature from that point on, as Paul tells us in **Romans 5:12**: "Therefore, just as sin came into the world through one man, and death through sin, and so death spread to all men because all sinned."

Our first parents' sin made every person from that time on be born with inherent sin. **First Corinthians 15:21-23** says, "For as by a man came death, by a man has come also the resurrection of the dead. For as in Adam all die, so also in Christ shall all be made alive. But each in his own order: Christ the firstfruits, then at his coming those who belong to Christ."

As Paul says in his letter to the church in Rome, we are all born with a sinful nature that is unrighteous, lacking in understanding, and having no inclination to seek God. **Romans 3:10-18** says:

> "None is righteous, no, not one; no one understands; no one seeks for God. All have turned aside; together they have become worthless; no on does good, not even one." "Their throat is an open grave; they use their tongues to deceive." "The venom of asps is under their lips." "Their mouth is full of curses and bitterness." "Their feet are swift to shed blood; in their paths are ruin and misery, and the way of peace they have not known. "There is no fear of God before their eyes."

Our flesh is indeed hostile to God as we see in **Romans 8:5, 7**: "For those who live according to the flesh set their minds on the things of the flesh . . . the mind that is set on the flesh is hostile to God, for it does not submit to God's law; indeed, it cannot." David also talks about being sinful from the womb in **Psalm 51:5** and **Psalm 58:3**. *Easton's Bible Dictionary* says this about our first parents' sin:

> Adam was constituted by God the federal head and representative of all his posterity, as he was also their natural head, and therefore when he fell they fell with him (Romans 5:12-21; 1 Corinthians 15:22-45); His probation was their probation, and his fall their fall. Because of Adam's first sin all his posterity came into the world in a state of sin and condemnation, i.e., (1) a state of moral corruption, and (2) of guilt, as having judicially imputed to them the guilt of Adam's first sin.[15]

Augustine coined the term "original sin" to refer to the origin of our sin nature. The assertion of original sin makes the point that we are not sinners *because* we sin, but rather we sin *because* we are sinners, born with a nature enslaved to sin.

We are born in total depravity. Does this mean we are as bad as we possibly could be? No. But it does mean that there is no part of us that is not touched by sin. The result is that no action of ours is completely untouched by it either—even the things we do that are considered "good." There is always some

---

15 M.G. Easton, *Illustrated Bible Dictionary*, New York: Cosimo Classics, 2005.

element of sin laced in with it, whether that sin is pride, self-righteousness, or wanting to look good to others. All of our best deeds are tainted, not to mention the bad things we do. There is no way for us to meritoriously earn God's favor.

There is a depth of darkness in our nature. We are, by nature, "children of wrath" (**Eph. 2:3**), who are "dead in our sin," as **Colossians 2:13 (NIV)** tells us. How sinful are we? As we read earlier in **Romans 3:10-18**, we are so sinful that we have no inclination to seek God. What does that mean for us? That we are so dead in our sin that we don't—in fact we *can't*—reach out to God to be saved. We are effectively "as dead as a door nail." We can do nothing to save ourselves.

Chapter 4

BOUND TO SIN THEN FREED TO LIVE RIGHTEOUSLY

So, what's a person to do now? How can someone who's dead do anything to help themselves at all? A dead man cannot restart his own heart, nor can he reach his hand out to try to do anything. He can't even ask for help. He's dead. Silent. Motionless. Utterly helpless. What he needs is someone to restart his heart for him. Spiritually, this is what we need, too, before we can do anything at all.

BOUND TO SIN

From the point of Adam and Eve's first sin, we no longer have the possibility to live "good enough" to please God. Adam and Eve started out living under a covenant of works (the ability to live pleasingly to God). However, from the moment of the Fall, every human being needs a covenant of grace. We need saving. So how, exactly, does a dead man get saved?

What must happen is God has to regenerate our stony, dead hearts *in order to make us able* to respond to the Gospel message when we hear it. We see one example of God doing this with Lydia in **Acts 16:13b-14**: "And we sat down and spoke to the women who had come together. One who heard us was a woman named Lydia, from the city of Thyatira, a seller of purple goods, who was a worshiper of God. The Lord opened her heart to pay attention to what was said by Paul."

This is exactly what God does, through the work of the Holy Spirit—He regenerates the hearts of the elect, while they are still dead. **Ephesians 2:1-9** says:

> And you were dead in the trespasses and sins, in which you once walked, following the course of this world, following the prince of the power of the air, the spirit that is now at work in the sons of disobedience—among whom we all once lived in the passions of our flesh, carrying out the desires of the body and the mind, and were by nature children of wrath, like the rest of mankind. But God, being rich in mercy, because of the great love with which he loved us, even when we were dead in our trespasses, made us alive together with Christ—by grace you have been saved—and raised us up with him and seated us with him in the heavenly places in Christ Jesus, so that in the coming ages he might show the immeasurable riches of his grace in kindness toward us in Christ Jesus. For by grace you have been saved through faith. And this is not your own doing; it is the gift of God, not a result of works, so that no one may boast.

We also see this is a gift from God, through the work of the Holy Spirit, in **1 Peter 1:1-2**: "To those who are elect exiles of the Dispersion in Pontus, Galatia, Cappadocia, Asia, and Bithynia, according to the foreknowledge of God the Father, in the sanctification of the Spirit, for obedience to Jesus Christ and sprinkling with his blood."

This foreknowledge is not God looking down through history to see who chooses Him. 9;This is not God expressing prior knowledge of facts about peoples' *choices*; it is foreknowledge, (which means forelove) of a person. It is God Who takes the initiative, not us. First, He chooses some to show His mercy to, as seen in **Romans 8:28-30**:

> And we know that for those who love God all things work together for good, for those who are called according to his purpose. For

those whom he foreknew he also predestined to be conformed to the image of his Son, in order that he might be the firstborn among many brothers. And those whom he predestined he also called, and those whom he called he also justified, and those whom he justified he also glorified.

We see this again in **2 Thessalonians 2:13 (AMP)**, where Paul says, "Because God has chosen you from the beginning for salvation" and in **Colossians 3:12**, where the elect are called "God's chosen ones, holy and beloved." **Ephesians 1:4-6** summarizes God's choice in election: "Even as he chose us in him before the foundation of the world, that we should be holy and blameless before him. In love he predestined us for adoption to himself as sons through Jesus Christ, according to the purpose of his will, to the praise of his glorious grace, with which he has blessed us in the Beloved."

It is up to God to whom He shows mercy. As God says in **Exodus 33:19**, "I will be gracious to whom I will be gracious, and I will show mercy on whom I will show mercy." God chose the people He would save (the elect) before the foundation of the world for His own reasons, and we aren't told why. This seems unfair to us as humans. It should seem unfair; grace is not fair. If it was, it would not be grace; it would be something we deserved. And no sinful human being deserves mercy from a perfectly holy God. This may be a hard concept to understand, or even to believe, if you've never heard it before. However, it is God's electing love that saves people the whole way through the entire Bible—Old and New Testaments. God chooses the people He saves. None of them save themselves; none of them ever could. The Bible says so. God always takes the initiative.

S-I-N IS THE REASON JESUS SUFFERED AND DIED

The second way God took the initiative was by sending His Son to die in our place, and He did it while we were too weak to help ourselves due to our ungodliness. "For while we were still weak, at the right time Christ died for the ungodly" (**Rom. 5:6**).

Hebrews 9:22 tells us, "Without the shedding of blood there is no forgiveness of sins." We see this shedding of blood throughout the Old Testament. First, with God shedding the blood of an animal to clothe Adam and Eve; then with Abel offering the first of his flock's fat portions; then with Noah sacrificing after they get off the ark; then Abraham getting ready to sacrifice Isaac, and God providing an animal sacrifice in Isaac's place; and from then on, until Jesus' death on the cross as the final, sacrificial, perfect Lamb of God Who, according to John the Baptist, "takes away the sin of the world" (**John 1:29**). So, our sin requires blood. It should be ours. For those who belong to Jesus, it is His instead.

In **Romans 3:23**, we are told, "For all have sinned and fall short of the glory of God." We are also told, "None is righteous, no, not one" (**Rom. 3:10**). To humans who think of themselves as "basically good" and self-sufficient, the idea of sin and needing a Savior can be a huge stumbling block. But if we think of sin as something less than it is, we will misunderstand the Good News of Jesus Christ. **And if we present the Gospel without explaining sin and separation from God, we are not presenting the Gospel of Jesus Christ**.

Matthew 20:26-28 says, "But whoever would be great among you must be your servant, and whoever would be first among you must be your slave—even as the Son of Man came not to be served but to serve, and to give his life as a ransom for many." Jesus came to pay the ransom price (the debt) we owed God for our sin. He also came to restore our broken relationship with God, as we're told in **1 Timothy 2:5-6**: "For there is one God, and there is one mediator between God and men, the man Christ Jesus, who gave himself as a ransom for all, which is the testimony given at the proper time." We also need to realize that the "cup" Jesus asks to be taken from Him in the Garden of Gethsemane is the *cup of God's wrath* (**Matt. 26:39**). As we know, He does willingly submit to the Father and accept the cup in our place. Jesus took God's wrath, which we deserved.

Why are we talking about all of this in a book about understanding the complete Gospel message? As unpopular as it is to talk about our need for Jesus because of our sin and our insufficiency at being able to please God on our own merit, it is very, very popular today to sell books, do Bible studies, and give sermons about a whole host of things Jesus came to do for us that have nothing to do with our sin and insufficiency. Dear Christian, Jesus did NOT come to give you a bigger, better life than you have now. You are not promised that! If Christians are promised anything in this life, it's suffering. As Paul tells the Philippian Church in **Philippians 1:29-30**: "For it has been granted to you that for the sake of Christ you should not only to believe in him but also suffer for his sake, engaged in the same conflict that you saw I had and now hear that I still have." He also tells the Corinthian church the same thing in **2 Corinthians 1:2-10**.

Likewise, we're promised trials, as we see in **James 1:2**: "Count it all joy, my brothers, when you meet trials of various kinds." And we're promised persecution, as we see in **Romans 8:35-36**: "Who shall separate us from the love of Christ? Shall tribulation, or distress, or persecution, or famine, or nakedness, or danger, or sword? As it is written, 'For your sake we are being killed all the day long; we are regarded as sheep to be slaughtered.'" These are only a few places we are told these things.

Furthermore, Jesus did not come to save us from a seemingly purposeless life, to save us from loneliness, or to fix the bad circumstance in our lives. You may even be a victim of someone else who caused horrific things in your life. Tragic though they are, these things are the effects of living in a fallen, sinful world. These effects are not your sin, though. You still need to be saved from your own sin. There's no promise Jesus is going to make all the bad stuff better in this life. We, as believers, are promised that "God will [someday] wipe away every tear from [our] eyes" in **Revelation 7:17** and **Revelation 21:4**, but offering someone who's hurting that promise is not the same as offering them the Gospel because it is not the Gospel.

Similarly, Jesus did not die just to be our Friend; He died to be our Savior! Our greatest need isn't a Friend; it's a Savior!

Not to belabor the point, but God is not searching for us, hoping to someday find us and make us His. He knows exactly where we are and what we're doing (omniscient), and He is right there with us (omnipresent). Most importantly (for this topic anyway), He's the Almighty, Omnipotent Ruler of All! Our broken relationship with God is not like any other relationship here on Earth. This broken relationship is total rebellion on our part, against our perfectly holy Creator. It deserves judgement and wrathful punishment.

Do these truths make you rethink how you share the Gospel with others? Do they make you rethink how you understand the Gospel message yourself? Do you know anyone who may be trusting in a false gospel that has nothing to do with dealing with their sin before God?

Sin brings ruin and misery. For a visual picture, you can think of the city of Sin—a city in ancient Egypt, called by the Greeks *Pelusium*, which means, as does also the Hebrew name, "clayey" or "muddy," so called from the abundance of clay found there.[16] It is called by Ezekiel "the stronghold of Egypt" (**Ezek. 30:15-16**), thus denoting its importance as a fortified city. It has been identified with the modern Tineh, "a miry place," where its ruins are to be found.[17] Of its boasted magnificence, only four red granite columns remain and some few fragments of others. This is a picture of us. We are stuck in the miry pit of the destruction of our sin and its consequences. The only way out is for God to show us mercy and pull us out and set us firmly on the Rock of Jesus.

GOD WILL HOLD EVERYONE ACCOUNTABLE

Romans 3:19 tells us that one day, "every mouth may be stopped, and the whole world may be held accountable to God." Sin results in death—spiritual

---
16   Ibid.
17   Ibid.

death, not just physical. Sin brings a separation from our perfectly holy God—our holy, holy, holy God! (**Isa. 59:2**).

Hell is real. God's righteous condemnation and deprivation of all that is valuable, pleasant, and worthwhile will be the nature of the experience of Hell (**Rom. 2:8-9**). But that is not all. Hell is unending, conscious punishment. The book of Jude clearly says this in its warning against false teaching in **Jude 5-13**, and it is described this way in **Revelation 20:9-10** as well. "God is a consuming fire," according to **Hebrews 12:29**.

The New Testament teachings about Hell should horrify us. It is supposed to. Here is a list of other verses that talk about Hell: **Isaiah 59:18-29; Matthew 5:22, 8:12, 13:41-42, 49-50, 18:9, 22:13, 24:50-51, 25:30, 41-46; Luke 16:22-28; 1 Thessalonians 5:3; 2 Thessalonians 1:6-9; 2 Peter 3:4-7; and Revelation 20:11-15**.

Hell is what we all deserve because of sin. We need a Savior. And that is why Jesus came and died—to be our Savior.

This chapter probably seems like a downer. It's supposed to. We cannot believe less than this ourselves if we are to really be saved. Sin and separation from God are our problem. It's why Jesus came and died. And we cannot leave this out or make it sound less than what it is when we present the Gospel, or we are preaching a false gospel. To do so would mean missing the boat. There is very good news in the Gospels! But you have to get the full understanding of the bad news first, to really understand the Good News. And when you have a complete and correct understanding of the bad news, the Good News will seem even better than you ever dared to think, hope, or imagine!

So, what happens when Jesus does become our Savior?

FREED TO LIVE RIGHTEOUSLY

Colossians 2:13 says, "And you, who were dead in your trespasses and the uncircumcision of your flesh, God made alive together with him." We no longer have the ability to not sin—unless we are saved by Jesus Christ! We are in bondage to sin, up until that point, and only after being saved are we freed to choose righteousness. Only then can we have a heart that is inclined to live pleasing to God.

In **Romans 7**, Paul says before we were saved, "we [bore] fruit for death" (verse five). But after our conversion, we are freed from our bondage to sin and able to do good through the Holy Spirit. This bondage, God tells us, is something He frees us from Himself (it's not our own doing).

We see this in **Psalm 51:10**, when David asks God, "Create in me a clean heart, O God, and renew a right spirit within me." In **Ezekiel 36:26-27**, God promised to change the hearts of His people Israel: "And I will give you a new heart, and a new spirit I will put within you. And I will remove the heart of stone from your flesh and give you a heart of flesh. And I will put my Spirit within you and cause you to walk in my statutes and be careful to obey my rules."

God does it this way for our good and for His glory. Promises of being freed from the tyranny of sin can be seen in other places in Scripture, such as **John 8:34-36** and **Romans 6:6**. This is what we're freed from; this is what we're talking about when we say "our chains are broken." We are freed from being bound to our sinful nature, and we are freed to live righteously—just like our first parents were originally. Will we do it perfectly from that time on? No. But through the work of the Holy Spirit, we will be more and more sanctified (made more and more holy) throughout the rest of our lives here on Earth. Praise God for the glorious work He does in us!

Chapter 5
1 + 1 = 1

Hearing that we are not just imperfect people who mess up occasionally, but are, instead, enemies of God and objects of His wrath, deserving damnation in Hell for eternity, can be a lot for someone to take in; but it is absolutely necessary for understanding the true Gospel message. And now that we have a handle on the bad news, we can start to look at the good news of the Gospel—Jesus has redeemed His people!

As we said previously, you don't want to give a less-than-accurate picture of the Gospel when witnessing to people. We certainly wouldn't want to stop after telling someone how serious their sin is and *not* tell them there is hope for them! The Gospel writers understood this. They all came out of the gate swinging, telling of the only One Who is capable of delivering this good news of hope.

- **Matthew 1:1**—"The book of the genealogy of Jesus Christ, the son of David, the son of Abraham." Writing to the Jewish people, Matthew immediately shows the genealogy of Jesus. He is showing the Jews that Jesus is the Messiah Who was promised throughout the Old Testament to come from the line of Abraham and David.

- **Mark 1:1**—"The beginning of the gospel of Jesus Christ, the Son of God." Mark is writing to the Romans, who understood power. He is identifying Jesus as the Son of the one, true God, so the readers would understand Jesus' power and authority.

- **Luke 1:31-33**—"And behold, you will conceive in your womb and bear a son, and you shall call his name Jesus. He will be great and will be called the Son of the Most High. And the Lord God will give to him the throne of his father David, and he will reign over the house of Jacob forever, and of his kingdom there will be no end." Luke is writing his Gospel to the Gentiles. In the midst of Jesus' birth narrative, Luke quotes the angel Gabriel to show Gentiles exactly Who this Baby was and what His significance would be.

- **John 1:1-4**—"In the beginning was the Word, and the Word was with God, and the Word was God. He was in the beginning with God. All things were made through him, and without him was not anything made that was made. In him was life, and the life was the light of men." John was writing to show all, especially new believers and unbelievers, that Jesus is God. His Gospel starts by showing that Jesus has existed for all time and that everything was made through Him. By calling Jesus "the Word," John is showing that Jesus is God revealed. Everything written about God's redemptive plan in Scripture comes to fulfillment in Jesus.

As with God the Almighty Father and Creator, before we delve into what Jesus has done for us, we need to have a foundational understanding of Who He is.

JESUS—FULLY MAN / FULLY GOD

So often we say Jesus became Man. While this is true, in no way did becoming Man mean Jesus gave up His Divine nature. When Jesus was born of Mary, He was in every way fully a human baby; but He was also in every way fully God. He had to be fully human to stand in the place of humans and pay the debt humans owed God. However, Jesus also needed to be fully

God, so He could defeat Satan and death. If Jesus had been just a Man, He would have not had the power to save us. If He were just God, He wouldn't have been a satisfactory sacrifice to pay the price for our sins.

When we put the doctrine of the Trinity (Jesus is fully God) and the doctrine of the Incarnation (Jesus is fully Man) together, we get that Jesus Christ is fully God and fully man, yet one Person. As J.I. Packer has said, "Here are two mysteries for the price of one—the plurality of persons within the unity of God, and the union of Godhead and manhood in the person of Jesus . . . Nothing in fiction is so fantastic as is this truth of the Incarnation."[18]

CHALCEDONIAN CREED

So important was the truth of Jesus, fully God being incarnated to fully Man, that the early Church considered it one of the premier tenants of Christian faith. From October 8-November 1, 451, the heads of the churches met in Chalcedon (now Istanbul, Turkey). There, they discussed two major issues:

1) The Nature of God and the Trinity

2) The Nature of Jesus as Human and Divine (called Christology).[19]

Out of this council came the Chalcedonian Creed. This creed has been the basis of orthodox Christianity since it was formulated. There are a total of twenty-eight canons in this creed, but here is the summary of what it says about Christology:

1. Jesus has two natures that are both full and complete—He is fully God, and He is fully Man.

---

18   J.I. Packer, *Concise Theology: A Guide to Historic Christian Beliefs*, Wheaton, IL: Tyndale House Publishers, Inc., 1993.
19   "Chalcedonian Creed," Theopedia.com, accessed October 15, 2018, https://www.theopedia.com/chalcedonian-creed.

2. Each nature is distinct—one nature does not change or take away from the other nature in any way.

3. Christ is only one Person—Both natures exist in the one person of Christ. Jesus cannot split His natures and become two separate beings.[20]

Today, all orthodox Christian and Catholic sects accept the Chalcedonian Creed as truth. A proper understanding of these truths clears up a lot of confusion and difficulties we may have in our minds. How can Jesus be both God and Man? Why doesn't this make Him two people? How does His Incarnation relate to the Trinity? How could Jesus have hungered and died when He was on Earth, and yet still be God? Did Jesus give up any of His Divine attributes in the Incarnation? Why is it wrong to say that Jesus is a "part" of God? Is Jesus still human now, and does He still have His human body? Did God die on the cross? Let's try and answer these questions.

1 + 1 = 1

Ask most Christians if they believe Jesus was fully Man and fully God, and they will say, "Of course!" But do they have a correct understanding of what this means? The two natures of Jesus are distinct and have their own properties. They do not alter one another's essential properties, and they do not mix together into a kind of third nature.

Jesus is God and has always been God. However, Jesus was not always Man. He became human at the Incarnation (His birth). Yet even after becoming fully human, He was still fully God. Both natures existed simultaneously within the Person of Jesus. Christ gave up none of His Divine attributes when He became Man; instead, He voluntarily limited Himself to using them. He chose to walk everywhere, even though He could have easily transported Himself anywhere He wanted to go. He made the choice to be limited to His

---

20 Ibid.

physical, fleshly confines. He decided to deal with His hunger, weariness, and thirst in the same way we would. And while He performed many miracles, never did He use His divine powers for His own needs.

He chose to experience humanity just as we do so that we would have a Savior Who could empathize with us. As **Hebrews 4:15** tells us, "For we do not have a high priest who is unable to sympathize with our weaknesses, but one who in every respect has been tempted as we are, yet without sin." This passage makes it clear that because Jesus became fully human, He can empathize with our weaknesses. In every other religion, the god or gods are far above and removed from the people. It is only Christianity that has the one, true God Who comes to Earth fully human to not only save His people, but also to empathize with them! No matter what we are facing, Jesus has faced it, too. That should be a huge encouragement to us!

Scripture makes it clear that Jesus has all of the human attributes. He has a human body—"concerning his Son, who was descended from David according to the flesh" (**Rom. 1:3**). He has a human mind—"And Jesus increased in wisdom and in stature and in favor with God and man" (**Luke 2:52**). He has human feelings and needs—"On the following day, when they came from Bethany, he was hungry" (**Mark 11:12**). Finally, He has a human soul—"My soul is very sorrowful, even to death" (**Matt. 26:38**).

It is important to understand the false views of Jesus. Understanding what we should not believe helps us better understand what we should believe. At the Council of Chalcedon, they rejected the notion that Christ has a human body, but not a human mind or spirit. The claim was that while Jesus was physically a Man, His mind and spirit were not human. In these two areas, He was only fully God. The Council rejected this notion because it denies that Jesus is fully Man. Instead, it presents Him as partially Man, with just a human body, while His mind and spirit were Divine.

Jesus does not just look like a man. He does not just have some aspects of humanity. He is a Man! He has all the essential elements of human nature: a human body, a human soul, a human mind, a human will, human needs, and human emotions. Because this is true, it is heresy to say things like, "Jesus is God with skin on," or "Jesus was a Man, but had the mind of God." He was, and is, just as human as the rest of us in every way, except one.

The one way Jesus was unlike every person who has ever lived since Adam and Eve is that He was born *without* a sin nature. Like Adam and Eve, He had the ability to *not* sin. But, unlike Adam, Jesus did not fail and was able to live in complete obedience to God. This is why He is called "the second Adam." **Romans 5:19** tells us, "For as by one man's disobedience the many were made sinners, so by the one man's obedience the many will be made righteous."

In order to succeed where the first Adam failed, Jesus needed to begin in the same place that Adam did. Because of our inborn sin nature, we are dead in our sin until and unless the Holy Spirit regenerates our hearts. If Jesus had been just another human, born with that same sin nature, it would have been like one dead man trying to save another.

Jesus became Man so that He could die for our sins. He had to *be* Human in order to pay the penalty *for* humans. He had to be a perfect Human, so He would be a sufficient Sacrifice for all of His people for all of time. Up until the time Christ came to Earth, animals were sacrificed in ceremonies to pay for the sins of the people. Even though the animals chosen were perfect and without defect, they were still so inadequate that they worked only temporarily. The sacrifice ritual needed to be repeated on a regular basis. This shows us that nothing we could do could ever be good enough to reconcile ourselves with God, and that was exactly God's intention. He let humans fail for a while, so we could see that we could never succeed on our own and that we desperately needed for Him to redeem us. (We will look into this deeper in the next chapter.)

Jesus was the ultimate, spotless Lamb Who was sacrificed as the Penalty for our sin on the cross. Understand, though, that it was Jesus' human nature that died on the cross. Therefore, we should never speak of Jesus' death as the death of God. Humans die; God cannot. But what we can say is that although it was Jesus' human nature that died, somehow His Divine nature also experienced death because of the union of the two natures.

How Jesus' two natures interact is a mystery—one that our finite minds cannot possibly fully understand. Let me show you what I mean. In **Matthew 24:36**, Jesus says about His return, "But concerning the day and hour no one knows, not even the angels of heaven, nor the Son, but the Father only." Jesus is God. It seems strange that He wouldn't know the day He would be returning to Earth. Sounds like either there is a discrepancy in Scripture, or Jesus was not being completely truthful with His disciples. Neither is the case. Jesus' two natures are separate and distinct. His Human nature is not omniscient. Jesus, fully Man, did not know the day or hour of His return. His Divine nature, however, *is* omniscient, so Jesus, fully God, did know when He would return. Since the two natures are united in one Person, Jesus both knew and didn't know the time of His return! In His human nature, the Person of Christ was unaware as to when He would return. In His Divine nature, the Person of Christ did know when He would return. Thus, Jesus both knew and didn't know when He would return! While this is a hard concept to grasp, it is an incredible phenomena! Head hurt? You are not alone!

ONE MAN, TWO NATURES, FOR ALL ETERNITY

For most people, it is obvious that Jesus will be God forever. But it may not be obvious that He will also be a Man forever. Some think that Jesus was only a Man during His time on Earth. This is not true. Jesus is still fully Man right now and will be for eternity. The Bible is clear that Jesus rose physically from the dead in the same body that had died. **Luke 24:39** says, "See my hands and my feet, that it is I myself! Touch me and see. For a spirit does not have flesh and bones as you see I have." And He ascended into Heaven as a

Man in His physical body. **Luke 24:50–51** says, "And he led them out as far as Bethany, and lifting up his hands he blessed them. While he blessed them, he parted from them and was carried up into heaven." It would make no sense for Jesus to have ascended bodily into Heaven, if He was simply going to ditch His body and stop being Man when He arrived in Heaven.

That Christ continued being Man with a physical body after His ascension is confirmed by the fact that when He returns, He will be as a Man in His body. He will return physically. **First Corinthians 15:42 and 2 Corinthians 5:1** tell us that both Jesus and all Christians will then continue living together in their bodies forever because the resurrection body cannot die, since it is eternal.

We jump ahead, though. Now that we have an understanding of Who Jesus is, let's look at what He did!

Chapter 6

PROMISES KEPT

"For our sake he made him to be sin who knew no sin, so that in him we might become the righteousness of God" (**2 Cor. 5:21**).

> *Behold Him there the risen Lamb*
> *My perfect spotless righteousness*
> *The great unchangeable I am*
> *The King of glory and of grace*
> *One with Himself I cannot die*
> *My soul is purchased by His blood*
> *My life is hid with Christ on high*
> *With Christ my Savior and my God!*[21]

This beautiful verse and song excerpt makes for a perfect transition from Who Jesus is to what Jesus did!

JESUS CHRIST, THE PROMISED MESSIAH

The name Jesus is the Greek form of Joshua, or *Yeshua*, meaning "God saves." The name Christ is the Greek equivalent of *Messiah*, which means "anointed deliverer." So, Jesus Christ means "God saves through an anointed deliverer." While the Gospel writers specifically name Jesus as that Anointed

---

21   Charitie Lees Bancroft, "Before the Throne of God Above," Northern Ireland, 1860, Public Domain.

Deliverer, it is certainly not the first time He is mentioned in Scripture. The Messiah is prophesied about throughout the Old Testament, beginning way back in **Genesis 3:15**: "I will put enmity between you and the woman, and between your offspring and her offspring; he shall bruise your head, and you shall bruise his heel." We talked about the Fall of Adam and Eve in the previous chapters. This verse comes after Adam and Eve have sinned. God is declaring the punishment on the serpent (Satan), who deceived Eve and led Adam and Eve into rebellion against God. This verse, aside from John 3:16, has been called the most important verse in the Bible. In fact, Genesis 3:15 is referred to as the *proto-evangelium* (the first Gospel) because it is the first mention of God's intention to redeem His people following the Fall in the Garden of Eden.

As we have learned, God should have destroyed Adam and Eve for their sin. It was the *just* thing to do. Instead, He shows that He has a plan of redemption in place for them and for all of His people for all time. Jesus is the One Whose heel will be struck by the serpent (Satan). This is a foreshadowing of the crucifixion. Jesus, by becoming human, puts Himself within reach of Satan. Notice God says Satan will strike Jesus' heel. This is a picture that Jesus will be in the position to be wounded by Satan and that He will shed blood as substitutionary blood for His people. God is saying that although Jesus will be struck, it will be a non-fatal blow. In contrast to that, Jesus will ultimately crush Satan's head by dealing a mortal blow to Satan and to death when He is resurrected. Satan throws his worst at Jesus—death. But neither death, nor Satan, can hold Him. Christ destroys both. Because of what our Savior did, Satan (the accuser of people before God) and death (the punishment for sin) are not just rendered completely defeated against Jesus Himself, but also against all of those who belong to Jesus! As Paul tells believers in **Romans 8:38-39**, "Neither death nor life, nor angels nor rulers, nor things present nor things to come, nor powers, nor height nor depth, nor anything else in all creation, will be able to separate us from the love of God in Christ Jesus our Lord."

While it may not seem like Satan and death have been completely overthrown right now—after all, there is a lot of bad stuff going on in the world—rest assured, they have. However, even though Satan is defeated, (and Satan knows he is) Jesus is allowing him some reign on the earth right now, keeping him on a short leash. **Mark 1:27** says, "He (Jesus) commands even the unclean spirits, and they obey him."

Recall the story of Jesus' foretelling of Peter's denial (**Luke 22:31-32**). This is an excellent example to show us that Satan needs to ask permission from God before attacking anyone. And even then, he can attack only within the boundaries that God sets. The same is true today. Satan can do nothing without permission from God. Satan will only be allowed even this limited reign for a time, though. His fate was sealed in **Genesis 3:15**, came to fruition at the resurrection, and will come to completion when Jesus comes back. As **Revelation 20:10** tells us, "The devil who had deceived them was thrown into the lake of fire and sulfur where the beast and the false prophet were, and they will be tormented day and night forever and ever."

WHY COME WHEN HE DID

It may seem to us that a lot of heartache, pain, and suffering could have been avoided if God had sent Jesus to Earth right after the events of Genesis 3:15. But He didn't. In fact, He didn't come for roughly another four thousand years! The Old Testament shows us what was happening during most of those four thousand years. Over and over in the narratives in the Old Testament, God gives His people precepts, or commands, of how they are to live. As we said previously, these precepts were meant so that life would go well with them. If they were obeyed, there were blessings that came upon the people. If they were disobeyed, there were curses. Time and time again, God's people are disobedient and, as a result, are punished. However, time and time again, God has mercy on them.

The main message of the Old Testament is that people cannot possibly save themselves from the wrath of God but need a perfect Savior to do it for them. The entire Old Testament points to Jesus! The theme of the Old Testament can be summed up as a picture of God's mercy and grace on His people that would ultimately come to fulfillment in Jesus Christ. Sixty-six books in the Bible, with approximately forty very different authors, were written over a period of seventeen hundred years, yet they all tell one continuous story of God's plan of redemption for His fallen people through Jesus, the Messiah.

Why did God wait for approximately four thousand years after the Fall to send Jesus to Earth? We don't know for sure, and the Bible does not give us any answers. One thing we do know, though, is that God knew before the foundation of the world exactly when Jesus would be sent. **Galatians 4:4-5** says, "But when the fullness of time had come, God sent forth his Son, born of woman, born under law, to redeem those who were under the law, so that we might receive adoption as sons." "When the fullness of time had come" tells us that the Trinity had pre-determined how long They would let the world exist with only the promise of a Messiah before that Messiah would physically appear.

We on this side of history have the privilege of seeing how desperate and desolate the world was without Jesus, without having to actually experience it. For God's people who lived up until Jesus' physical coming, they had to cling to the promises of the coming Messiah given to them through God's prophets:

- **Isaiah 9:2, 6-7**—"The people who walked in darkness have seen a great light; those who dwelt in a land of deep darkness, on them a light has shone . . . For to us a child is born, to us a son is given; and the government shall be upon his shoulder, and his name shall be called Wonderful Counselor, Mighty God, Everlasting Father, Prince of Peace. Of the increase of his government and of peace there will be no end, on the throne of David and over his kingdom, to establish it and to uphold it with justice and with righteousness from this time forth and forever more. The zeal of the Lord of hosts will do this."

- **Amos 9:11**—"In that day, I will raise up the booth of David that is fallen and repair its breaches, and raise up its ruins and rebuild it as in the days of old."

- **Zechariah 3:9**—"Declares the Lord of hosts, and I will remove the iniquity of this land in a single day."

These prophecies, and many others, were given to the Jewish people at various times in their history, but there was always one common factor. They were given at the times when the people needed hope. Although God punished them for their disobedience, He never left His people without hope and encouragement of a future time when He would send them a righteous King Who would deliver them and, once and for all, save them from their sin.

Although God decided not to divulge to the people of the Old Testament exactly when the Messiah would appear, we, again, on this side of history have an advantage. If you read secular history up until the time of Jesus' birth, you see many things that occurred that made it the perfect time for His Incarnation. You can't help but be amazed when you understand what was going on in the world during Old Testament times and the four hundred years between the Old and New Testament. It's like getting a behind-the-scenes glimpse into what God was doing to make the world ready for the coming of His Son!

One occurrence, though, can't help but trouble us. The Roman Empire, who was in control of most of the known world during Jesus' earthly life, kept the peace throughout their vast empire by using the most horrific and cruel methods of punishment in all of history. Jesus would be on the receiving end of this torture.

It seems puzzling to us why God would choose one of the most violent, brutal times in history to send Jesus. After all, Jesus just needed to shed blood, die in our place, and then be resurrected. We wonder why God did not allow Him to die in a more humane manner. The answer to that is not easy to hear. The suffering and torture Jesus endured is illustrative of the callousness and cruelty of Satan and of man. Satan's hatred of God and His Son, Jesus, may have been the motivation behind the extreme torture and abuse, but it is also an example of how unsaved man feels toward our Holy God. **Romans 3:12-18** tells us:

> "All have turned aside; together they have become worthless; no one does good, not even one." "Their throat is an open grave; they use their tongue to deceive." "The venom of asps is under their lips." "Their mouth is full of curses and bitterness." Their feet are swift to shed blood; in their paths are ruin and misery, and the way of peace they have not known." "There is no fear of God before their eyes."

Isaiah 53:3-5 shows how this godlessness of man translated into the suffering of Jesus:

> "He was despised and rejected by men, a man of sorrows and acquainted with grief; and as one from whom men hide their faces he was despised, and we esteemed him not. Surely he has borne our griefs and carried our sorrows; yet we esteemed him stricken, smitten by God, and afflicted. But he was pierced for our transgressions; he was crushed for our iniquities; upon him was the chastisement that brought us peace, and with his wounds we are healed."

We have already talked about how sinful we are, but these verses give us a look into just how ugly and dark our hearts are before we are saved.

PROMISES KEPT

Once you understand that the Old Testament ultimately points to Jesus, you can't help but see Him throughout the narratives. J. Barton Payne has made note of 574 passages in the Old Testament that are prophecies of the coming of Jesus.[22] Here are just a few examples:

- **Numbers 24:17**—"I see him, but not now; I behold him, but not near. A star shall come out of Jacob, and a scepter shall rise out of Israel."

- **Isaiah 7:14**—"Therefore the Lord himself will give you a sign. Behold, the virgin shall conceive and bear a son, and shall call his name Immanuel."

- **Micah 5:2**—"But you, O Bethlehem Ephrathah, who are too little to be among the clans of Judah, from you shall come forth for me one who is to be ruler in Israel, whose coming forth is from of old, from ancient days."

Over and over, God promises a Messiah that would once and for all put an end to despair and evil and rescue His people from their sin. If we use Payne's number of 574 prophecies about Jesus in the Old Testament, the probability of one man fulfilling them all isn't even a known mathematical number! (And we haven't even mentioned the many times Jesus physically or spiritually appears in the Old Testament!) Yet Jesus fulfilled every one of those prophecies, leaving no doubt He is the One Whom God, through the prophets, spoke of. Some of the prophecies are worded in such a way that no one, except Jesus, could have possibly fulfilled them.

For example, **Genesis 49:10** says, "The scepter shall not depart from Judah, nor the ruler's staff from between his feet, until tribute comes to him." The original Hebrew word for "ruler" is *chaqaq*, which means "lawgiver." Jesus is God and, as God, is the Giver of the law. Also, the prophecy says that Judah's tribe would remain the chief tribe in Israel until the

---

22 Walter C. Kaiser, Jr., "Jesus in the Old Testament," Gordon-Conwell Theological Seminary, accessed October 15, 2018, https://www.gordonconwell.edu/resources/Jesus-in-the-Old-Testament.cfm.

Messiah came. Judah was the chief tribe in Israel up to and including the time of Jesus' incarnation (Jesus is from the tribe of Judah). In 70 A.D., the Temple was destroyed, and any semblance of a scepter was gone from Judah. This means the Messiah couldn't possibly come after 70 A.D.

Some of the prophecies said that the Messiah would be from the lineage of Abraham and David. Thus when Jesus, Who is in the line of Abraham and David, arrived on the scene, there was great excitement amongst many Jews.

Discord began to arise, however, because many of the Jewish people who were initially excited about Jesus' coming did not understand what was written in Scripture. They interpreted the Old Testament prophecies to mean that a Messiah would deliver them from their earthly circumstances. The Jewish people were a battered people. Throughout their history, they were overthrown, oppressed, and taken captive by many nations. When Jesus arrived, the Jewish people were under control of the Roman Empire. Although the Romans let them practice their religion in relative peace, in 63 B.C., when they first took control of the Israelites, they massacred the Jewish priests right in the Temple. The Jewish people had not forgiven them for that and hated the Romans. The people were looking for a king to lead a rebellion and free them from their oppression once and for all. They did not grasp that the Kingdom Jesus came to establish was not of this world. Jesus, though, consistently and frequently corrects them, telling the Jewish people that He did not come to be an earthly king. One of these times is in **John 18:36**: "Jesus answered, 'My kingdom is not of this world. If my kingdom were of this world, my servants would have been fighting, that I might not be delivered over to the Jews. But my kingdom is not of this world."

Many Jewish people were looking for an earthly king to lead a revolution and defeat the oppressive Roman Empire, not a Divine King to lead them into the eternal Kingdom of God.

JESUS, THE SAVIOR FOR SINNERS

Jesus' ushering in the Kingdom of God is Good News indeed! However, there was still the problem of sin keeping people from God. Jesus not only came to inaugurate in the Kingdom of God, but also came to be the sacrificial offering for His people. He came to be punished in our place as *our* sin deserves. Thus, for those of us who are trusting in that sacrifice, He secures forgiveness for us from Almighty God, allowing us to live in peace with Him while we are on this Earth and when we are eternally with Him in Heaven.

God prepared His people for the coming Savior by sending John the Baptist. As **Luke 1:15-17** tells us about John the Baptist, "He will be filled with the Holy Spirit, even from his mother's womb. And he will turn many of the children of Israel to the Lord their God, and he will go before him in the spirit and power of Elijah . . . to make ready for the Lord a people prepared." John the Baptist was born for the purpose of announcing the coming of Jesus. "Behold the Lamb of God, who takes away the sin of the world" (**John 1:29**) was his message.

To the first century Jews, John's message was clear. It was a throw-back to Exodus, when the Israelites were delivered out of Egypt. God told them to sacrifice a perfect lamb, cook it, eat it, and wipe its blood on the doorways of their homes. That night, the angel of death came through all of Egypt; and any door without the blood on it would have the first-born male—both human and animal—killed. For those with the blood on the doorway, the angel of death "passed over" and spared the household. This historic event was something ingrained in Jewish history. The Jewish people would have understood the reference of Jesus as the ultimate Passover Lamb from God. When Jesus' blood is wiped on our hearts, the angel of death (God's wrath) passes over us.

As we said, many Jewish people rejected Jesus as the Messiah they thought they were looking for, but this was certainly not true of all of the

Jews. Jesus' twelve apostles were all Jewish. They, along with other followers, would go on to start the first churches. Even though Jesus shared His mission with His apostles several times while He was on Earth, it wasn't until after His resurrection that the apostles fully understood Who Jesus was and why He had come. How could we expect them to? First, what Jesus was telling them was so foreign to them, they couldn't comprehend it; and second, they needed the Holy Spirit to open their minds, so they could understand. Once this happened, the lightbulb went off! They became empowered and boldly preached the Gospel throughout the known world, even upon punishment of death. They understood the significance and purpose of Jesus' death as told to them by Jesus Himself in passages such as **Matthew 26:26-28** and **Mark 10:45**.

It was only due to the Holy Spirit that the apostles were able to understand what Jesus accomplished on the cross. The same is true for us. Without the Holy Spirit regenerating our hearts and opening our minds, we cannot possibly comprehend what Jesus did. In fact, to those without the Holy Spirit, it will all seem like nonsense.

> "What no eye has seen, nor ear heard, nor the heart of man imagined, what God has prepared for those who love him"—these things God has revealed to us through the Spirit. For the Spirit searches everything, even the depths of God . . . The natural person does not accept the things of the Spirit of God, for they are folly to him, and he is not able to understand them because they are spiritually discerned (**1 Cor. 2:9-10, 14**).

CONCLUSIONS

Here is the bottom line: We are the ones who should have died, not Jesus. We should have been punished, not Him. And yet He took our place and died for us. "They were my transgressions, but His wounds. My iniquities, but his chastisement. My sin, His sorrow. And His punishment bought my peace. His stripes won my healing. His grief, my joy. His death, my life."[23]

In theological terms, this is called "substitutionary atonement." Christ died on the cross as our Substitute. Without Him, we would suffer the death and damnation penalty for our own sins. God forsook His own Son so that He might never have to forsake His children.

Substitutionary atonement is usually the part of the Gospel people buck at—even some who profess to be Christians. Some find the whole concept of the crucifixion and being washed by blood barbaric. Others are offended at the suggestion that they needed Someone to die for them and that they can't save themselves. There are even *other* theories among Christians as to why Jesus died on the cross.

One is the **Moral-Influence Theory**. First suggested by Peter Abelard (1079-1142), this says that Jesus did not make a sacrificial payment to the Father in order to satisfy God's judgment. Instead, Jesus wanted to demonstrate the full extent of God's love for the human race. Thus, the primary reason for Jesus' death was not to uphold God's honor, but to relieve the feelings of fear and alienation humans feel toward God. They use 2 Corinthians 5:19 as their basis: "That is, in Christ God was reconciling the world to himself, not counting their trespasses against them, and entrusting to us the message of reconciliation." Advocates of this theory like to emphasize God's love while downplaying His justice, holiness, and righteousness. They argue, ultimately, the show of Jesus' love on the cross will lead people to repentance.

Another theory is called the **Ransom Theory**. This was actually the standard theory in the early Church. It was the dominant theory until around 1033 A.D. They use Mark 10:45: "For even the Son of Man came not to be served but to serve, and to give his life as a ransom for many." Their premise is that human beings are enslaved to Satan. Satan demanded a ransom from God

---

23 The Significance of Isaiah 53:4-5 meme, *Me.me*, @PoppaFrank, https://me.me/i/the-significance-of-isaiah-53-4-5-ultimately-it-means-that-im-16236657.

to set us free. God agreed and sent Jesus to be that Ransom. Satan thought Jesus became totally human (dropped all of His Divine attributes) when He came to Earth. God kept the fact that Jesus was still fully God from Satan, so He could trick him into thinking that he could actually kill Jesus. Satan was shocked and horrified when Jesus was resurrected.

While both of these theories have threads of truth in them, neither is accurate, and both are a misrepresentation of God and Jesus and, therefore, heresy. The true substitutionary atonement doctrine is crucial to the Gospel message. Trying to preach the Gospel without it not only dishonors what Jesus did for us on the cross, but it will also leave people with more questions than answers!

In a sentence, Jesus died on the cross because He was the only satisfactory Sacrifice that could reconcile sinful man to a Holy God. Think of two cliffs across from each other. On the one side is us, and on the other is God. Between the two is a huge, deep chasm that is impossible to cross. Jesus is the only Bridge big enough to cover that chasm. Because of His taking our punishment, we can walk across the Bridge and approach our Heavenly Father. Instead of seeing us with our dark, ugly sin coming toward Him, God, instead, sees Jesus, His perfect, righteous Son, and welcomes us with open arms!

As beautiful as this picture is, we can't end the Gospel message with Jesus' sacrificial death. We must include His resurrection. If He hadn't been resurrected on the third day, He would have just been another great teacher, or perhaps a prophet who was martyred. Jesus' resurrection changed everything!

WHAT DOES JESUS' RESURRECTION MEAN FOR US?

First, and foremost, the fact that Jesus was resurrected shows He was fully God. His coming back to life is the victory over Satan, sin, and death. As we said, if He had just died, He would have been a martyr, and our condition would remain unchanged. It is His resurrection that gives His elect assurance that not only has God forgiven our sin, but we are also no longer enslaved to sin, Satan, or death. Just as Jesus prevailed over these, so we have, too, if we are His.

Second, the resurrection of Jesus shows that justice will prevail. We live in a society where justice is often perverted and/or neglected. The resurrection means that God's perfect justice will ultimately triumph. God will always prevail over evil!

Third, the resurrection assures our future resurrection. Because Jesus both died and rose again in body, we will be raised, in body, like Him. Jesus died and physically rose again; so, we know that our bodies will physically resurrect, in some way. To what extent, who knows? But if our resurrected body is like Jesus', it will mean that we will be clearly recognizable as He was to His disciples.

Fourth, the resurrection of Jesus initiated the coming of the Holy Spirit, which gives us the power to live out the Christian life. We have the living God not just with us, but in us!

We end this chapter as we began—with a song, courtesy of Elvina M. Hall, 1865:

> *I hear the Savior say,*
> *"Thy strength indeed is small;*
> *Child of weakness, watch and pray,*
> *Find in Me thine all in all."*
> *Jesus paid it all,*
> *All to Him I owe;*
> *Sin had left a crimson stain,*
> *He washed it white as snow.*
> *And now complete in Him,*
> *My robe, His righteousness,*
> *Close sheltered 'neath His side,*

I am divinely blest.
Lord, now indeed I find
Thy pow'r, and Thine alone,
Can change the leopard's spots
And melt the heart of stone.
And when before the throne
I stand in Him complete,
I'll lay my trophies down,
All down at Jesus' feet.
Jesus paid it all,
All to Him I owe;
Sin had left a crimson stain,
He washed it white as snow. [24]

---

[24] "Jesus Paid It All," words by Elvina M. Hall, music by John Grape, Public Domain, Baltimore, MD, 1865.

Chapter 7

"AND THE ANSWER IS . . ."

So, now that we've learned about Jesus, our Savior, the perfect Lamb of God, Who became our Substitute, Who took God's wrath on Himself for us, how do we respond? What is the proper response, the only *saving* response, to what Jesus has done? The answer is *faith*.

Faith is a word used a lot today. We have faith that a company will refund our money if their product fails to work as promised. We say we have faith that the medicine we've been prescribed will get rid of our sore throat. Often, we're told to "have faith," but without being told what to have it in.

Believe is a similar word. It's a synonym of faith. We're told to "just believe" that things will work out. Some people actually think that if they just have enough faith or enough belief, that their circumstances will turn out exactly the way they want them to.

But what does the Bible have to say about faith? What do we mean when we talk about having "saving faith"? What does it mean to have faith in God? What does it take to become a Christian? What happens once we are? If we've said the "sinner's prayer," are we really saved? If your parents baptized you as an infant, are you saved? How, exactly, should we respond to Jesus' death on the cross in order to be saved?

THE CHOSEN ARE REGENERATED AND CALLED

As we've talked about in the previous chapters, for God's elect, the Holy Spirit regenerates our stony hearts—at some point in our lives—and gives us a heart of flesh. We are, therefore, then able to—and, at some point, definitely will—respond to the Gospel message when we hear it. This response to what Jesus has done for us is usually associated with two words: *Faith* and *Repentance*.

Let's back up a bit and start at the point that our hearts are regenerated. In **Romans 8:30**, Paul refers to a "calling." This is not a calling as we would talk about being "called" into a job. It is the calling to those who were predestined and then had their hearts regenerated. It is the summons of the King of the universe that can't be denied and brings about the desired response in His people's hearts.

In other words, it is an act of God the Father, speaking through the human proclamation of the Gospel. This proclamation is a general calling of all people ("many are called"), but is only accepted by those whose hearts have been regenerated ("but few are chosen"—Matt. 22:14). It is the call in which the King summons His people to Himself, and they respond in saving faith. We call this "effectual calling."

Human preaching and teaching are the ways that the general Gospel call goes forth, as Paul writes about in **2 Thessalonians 2:13-14**: "But we ought always to give thanks to God for you, brothers beloved by the Lord, because God chose you as the firstfruits to be saved, through sanctification by the Spirit and belief in the truth. To this he called you through our gospel, so that you may obtain the glory of our Lord Jesus Christ."

This is why it's important to proclaim the Gospel message, trusting that God will, through His effectual call, bring His people to Him. This is why it's important, even though we believe in the doctrine of election, to spread the Gospel message. How else are God's elect going to hear it? Just because we know and believe that the elect will definitely be saved, that doesn't relinquish us of our responsibility and doesn't give us the right to keep our mouths shut when we could proclaim the Gospel!

Like we have said before, not all Gospel calls are effective. The job of believers is to explain the Gospel message, but it is up to God whether that message or call is effectual. It's important to understand that we are NOT responsible for "getting anyone saved"; nor are we responsible if someone dies without any evidence of salvation. We spread the Gospel out of obedience to God because we love Him, not because the pastor made us feel guilty that "Uncle Bob" never made a profession of faith before he died, as if it was our fault. We spread the Gospel to reach God's elect, not knowing who that may or may not be.

It's important to say here that infant regeneration can also be a reality if God so purposes. We see evidence of this with John the Baptist. In **Luke 1:15**, the angel tells Zechariah, the father of John the Baptist, that John would be filled with the Holy Spirit before he was even born! We see this is true when his mother, Elizabeth, was filled with the Holy Spirit after her baby leapt for joy in her womb when they came into the presence of the unborn baby Jesus (**Luke 1:41-44**). The doctrine of election is something we can take comfort in and help others take comfort in when we're talking about the possible salvation of those who cannot make a profession of faith on their own, including those who cannot hear or understand the Gospel and the unborn. When it is God doing the saving from start to finish, we have the hope that anyone can be saved.

But getting back to the response to the Gospel call: what happens when a heart is regenerated by the Holy Spirit and hears the Gospel message? If you're a Christian now, was there a time you remember when you heard the Gospel message or heard a sermon from the Bible, and something resounded in your heart that told you it was true? What happens in the heart? It believes! It has faith! But faith in what?

"AND THE ANSWER IS . . . FAITH ALONE (SOLA FIDE) IN CHRIST'S WORK ALONE (SOLO CHRISTO)!"

What is faith? Faith is, in general, the firm persuasion that a certain statement is true. But its primary idea here is trust. A thing is true and, therefore, worthy of trust. We often think of faith as believing in something you can't see or prove, and that is true as we're told in **Hebrews 11:1-13**, a solid reminder of the faith of the patriarchs. But it is more than that. Biblically speaking, faith is total reliance. Just as a skydiver totally relies on his parachute opening to save him from freefalling to the ground, the believer must totally rely on Jesus' finished work on the cross for salvation. The skydiver can't rely on flapping his arms (or anything else of his own) to stop his descent; he has nothing inside of himself to do it. True faith for salvation is the realization that you have absolutely nothing to offer to God on your own to save yourself, but you now have a firm belief and trust—a total reliance on—the risen Jesus to save you from sin and restore your relationship with God.

The greatest need of every human is that when we stand before God, He declares us "righteous" and not "condemned." When we trust in (have faith in) Jesus' death on the cross as atonement for our sin, we are declared righteous by God. "For Christ also suffered once for sins, the righteous for the unrighteous, that he might bring us to God, being put to death in the flesh but made alive in the Spirit" (**1 Peter 3:18**). In this instantaneous act, God declares our sins are forgiven, and Jesus' righteousness is imputed to us (we are clothed in it). In other words, the perfect life that Jesus lived is credited to us. We've become united to Jesus, and an exchange takes place. Just as we get credit for His perfect righteousness, all of our sinfulness is imputed (or credited) to Him; and He died and suffered God's wrath because of it.

If you are a Christian, have you ever thought about this exchange that took place? The reason God had to turn His face away from Jesus while

He was on the cross was because He saw *us* there! Jesus did not just suffer physically. In fact, that was probably the least of what He had to go through. His having to take on our sin and experience God's wrath and rejection was most likely far more painful than the nails and thorns. Having "saving faith" means receiving and resting on Christ and His righteousness by faith—a faith we do not have of ourselves, but "it is the gift of God" (**Eph. 2:8**). This faith is more than just wishful thinking or hopeful optimism. This faith is sure and established. It does *not* leave you wondering whether you will end up in the glorious presence of God in Heaven or suffering eternal punishment in Hell upon death. It does not leave you relying on your good works outweighing your bad. It leaves no room for boasting in your own merit, only room for boasting about what Christ has done.

This faith is the lone instrument of justification (being made in right relationship with God). **Romans 3:19-28** tells us there is no justification obtained for man through the law. Even those in the Old Testament times were not made righteous by the law. They, like us, needed the perfect sacrifice that Christ provided, which has now been revealed. They obtained it through faith in God's promises to them and faithfully looking expectantly forward to the coming Messiah. The law was given to show them that they could not keep it perfectly, and therefore, they needed a Savior. The temple sacrifices had to be done over and over again. This showed their need for a perfect Sacrificial Lamb to once and for all pay for their sin. They looked forward to His coming. We look back upon His finished work.

Justification is an instantaneous event that results in a permanent change of our status before God. Just like when a child is adopted into a family, the very moment the papers are signed and the adoption is finalized, the child is now a full-fledged member of the family. His status has changed *permanently*. And we, at the very second of justification, have a permanent status change. Sadly, many Christians don't live like this is a permanent reality. Instead, they live as if their status before God is changeable moment to moment, day to day, based on how their moral performance is going. The apostle Paul did not live this way! The status of being clothed in Christ's righteousness was a daily reality in His earthly life, and this is made plain for us in **Galatians 2:19-20**: "For through the law I died to the law, so that I might live to God. I have been crucified with Christ. It is no longer I who live, but Christ who lives in me. And the life I now live in the flesh I live by faith in the Son of God, who loved me and gave himself for me." Paul rested in the knowledge that he could never be pleasing enough to God, no matter how well he behaved, and that he didn't have to! Jesus had already lived perfectly for him. We should also rest in the assurance of this . . . daily.

Is this a license to sin, knowing that you'll be forgiven (antinomianism)? Certainly not! We are called to live righteously and to cooperate with the Holy Spirit to mortify our sin. Paul tells us this himself in **Romans 6:13-18**:

> Do not present your members to sin as instruments for unrighteousness, but present yourselves to God as those who have been brought from death to life, and your members to God as instruments for righteousness. For sin will have no dominion over you, since you are not under law but under grace. What then? Are we to sin because we are not under law but under grace? By no means! Do you not know that if you present yourselves to anyone as obedient slaves, you are slaves of the one whom you obey, either of sin, which leads to death, or of obedience, which leads to righteousness? But thanks be to God, that you who were once slaves of sin have become obedient from the heart to the standard of teaching to which you were committed, and, having been set free from sin, have become slaves of righteousness.

Christian, do you live your life on a roller coaster of ups and downs, thinking that God is either pleased with you or mad at you, depending on your behavior? If so, you can take heart in the assurance that your sins are paid for, and God sees you clothed in Christ's righteousness, even when you are at your worst. This is not a license to sin as much as you want to; but it is a truth that you can rest in!

Now that we have discussed the issue of faith being our response to the Gospel call, there are some other things to clear up.

BUT WHAT ABOUT REPENTANCE?

There is some debate about repentance being a necessary part of salvation, along with faith. The truth is, there really isn't anything all that debatable about it. Repentance is a fruit of faith, just as faith is a fruit of regeneration. All are gifts of God resulting from regeneration. If you have true faith, you will want to repent.

What is repentance? "The New Testament word for repentance means changing one's mind so that one's views, values, goals, and ways are changed, and one's whole life is lived differently."[25] Repentance means having a real change of heart and mind—one that makes you turn from your sinful ways and actually change how you live your life. Repentance begins with starting to loath your sin so much, that you actually don't want to live that way any longer, and you (with the help of the Holy Spirit) begin to mortify it.

The call to repent is found in the preaching of John the Baptist in **Matthew 3:1-2** when he said, "Repent, for the kingdom of heaven is at hand." It is preached by Jesus in **Matthew 4:17**: "From that time Jesus began to preach, saying, 'Repent, for the kingdom of heaven is at hand." We see it again preached by the Twelve, in **Mark 6:12**: "So they went out and proclaimed that people should repent." We find other examples by Peter at Pentecost in **Acts 2:38**; by Paul to the Epicureans and Stoics in Athens in **Acts 17:30**; when Paul is before King Agrippa in **Acts 26:20**; by the glorified Christ to the seven

---

25 J.I. Packer, *Concise Theology: A Guide to Historic Christian Beliefs*, Carol Stream, IL: Tyndale House Publishers, 1993.

churches in Asia in **Revelation 2:5, 16, 22**; and again, in **Revelation 3:3, 19**. Repentance is important!

Repentance is a turning away from sin and a turning toward positive behavior, including a willingness to make restitution to those we've personally sinned against where appropriate as shown to us in the Old Testament laws of **Exodus 22:3-14 and Leviticus 24:18-20**. Old Testament laws are important to us today because they were given to show what Kingdom life should look like. In other words, what it looks like to love God with all your heart, soul, and mind, and to "love . . . your neighbor as yourself" (**Luke 10:27**). The idea of turning away from sin and toward proper behavior is also seen in John the Baptist's words to the Pharisees and Sadducees who came to where he was baptizing: "Bear fruit in keeping with repentance" (**Matt. 3:8**). And we see Zacchaeus doing this in **Luke 19:8**: "And Zacchaeus stood and said to the Lord, 'Behold, Lord, the half of my goods I give to the poor. And if I have defrauded anyone of anything, I restore it fourfold.'"

A Christian will begin thinking of his sin as something he hates. He will cooperate with the Holy Spirit to mortify his sin. It will become despicable to him. He will grieve over his sin. To say "Jesus is my Savior" and yet not be willing to submit to Him as Lord over your life is nonsense. None of us easily submits ourselves to someone else—even to Jesus, Who spilled His precious blood to save us—as sad as it is to admit that! But make no mistake that a true Christian will have a contrite heart over his sin, a true remorse over having offended God. We see David's remorse over sleeping with Bathsheba in **Psalm 51:3-4**: "For I know my transgressions, and my sin is ever before me. Against you, you only, have I sinned and done what is evil in your sight, so that you may be justified in your words and blameless in your judgement." We see it with the prodigal son in **Luke 15:21**: "And the son said to him, 'Father, I have sinned against heaven and before you. I am no longer worthy to be called your son.'"

Psalm 51:15-17 says that God delights in a heart broken and contrite over sin. It is an unpopular concept to be "broken" in any way today, but this is what God delights in, in regard to our sin! True repentance is being broken and crushed by the weight of our sin because of its offense to God, turning to God for forgiveness, and having the *desire* to sin no more. We may (and probably will) still have the consequences of our sin to deal with, and we may still have sadness because of it; but we know that we can rest in the assurance that we are forgiven by God.

In the opposite sort of way, there is a type of repentance motivated by remorse, self-reproach, and sorrow for sin, generated by a fear of punishment. This is an incomplete repentance called attrition or "false repentance." It is a mere acknowledgment that sinners deserve to be punished but is lacking in an appeal to God for forgiveness and lacking in any intention of turning away from sin and striving against it.

One example of this is with Esau in **Genesis 27:30-38** and **Hebrews 12:17**. Esau did not seem to mind giving up his birthright for a bowl of stew until he realized the consequences of his actions. Only then was he sorry, and only because he was going to be missing out on the blessings that went with that birthright.

This manifests itself today in ways like saying the "sinner's prayer" to just buy "fire insurance" against Hell—thinking those words will protect you—or by running to the altar call or the baptism service over and over again because you're afraid God's mad at you. Or you may feel guilty because of the sins you've been committing lately when, in reality, you don't want to change—you just want to feel better for a while. These are just some examples. Jesus has *not* made atonement for those who are not truly repentant. Neither words alone nor baptism (not even baptism over and over again) will save you. Does this make you start to see why knowing the whole Gospel message is important? Do you see how an incomplete message could leave someone with a false sense of hope?

True repentance will come to those who are truly relying on Jesus in faith. Now, to finish this chapter, we need to take a look at some other ideas Christians have about what is needed to be saved.

BUT WHAT ABOUT BAPTISM? GOOD WORKS? AND SPEAKING IN TONGUES? DON'T I HAVE TO DO THESE TO BE SAVED?

Baptism is a means of grace; baptism cannot save you. Although Roman Catholics believe it does, the truth is, it doesn't. Parents in other denominations often have their infants baptized to make them part of the covenant community (same as Old Testament circumcision). We see evidences of these baptized infants growing up and eventually dying, sometimes saved and sometimes unsaved. Likewise, there are adults who get baptized, who never show any fruit in their lives and possibly (or probably) are unsaved. And there are adults who never get baptized, and yet, are saved. Baptism does not save.

Do we need good works in addition to our faith? The thief on the cross didn't have any time to do good works, and Jesus told him that he would be with Him in paradise. Good works are an expression of faith. This was the belief of the Reformers, including Luther, in that true faith would show itself by good works; it would produce fruit. Dead faith, just like a dead tree, would produce no fruit. Paul tells us that we are saved by grace, not works, in his letter to the Ephesian church in **Ephesians 2:8-10**: "For by grace you have been saved through faith. And this is not your own doing; it is the gift of God, not a result of works, so that no one may boast."

This passage goes on to tell us that God prepared our good works in advance in verse ten: "For we are his workmanship, created in Christ Jesus for good works, which God prepared beforehand, that we should walk in them."

Our deeds are never perfect anyway. They are always tainted with sin, as we see in **Isaiah 64:6**: "We have all become like one who is unclean, and all our righteous deeds are like a polluted garment. We all fade like a leaf, and our iniquities, like the wind, take us away." People say that James is making the argument that we need good works in **James 2:14-26**. But is James contradicting Paul (and others) who emphatically say that it's faith alone that saves? James is emphasizing that one does not need good works to be saved, but it does prove their salvation to be genuine. As commentator A. R. Fausset states:

> The question here is not as to the ground on which believers are justified, but about the demonstration of their faith: so in the case of Abraham. In Genesis 22:1 it is written, God did tempt Abraham, that is, put to the test of demonstration the reality of his faith, not for the satisfaction of God, who already knew it well, but to demonstrate it before men. The offering of Isaac at that time formed no part of the ground of his justification, for he was justified previously on his simply believing in the promise of spiritual heirs, that is, believers, numerous as the stars. He was then justified: that justification was showed or manifested by his offering Isaac forty years after. That work of faith demonstrated, but did not contribute to his justification. The tree shows its life by its fruits, but it was alive before either fruits or even leaves appeared.[26]

What James is combating here in this passage is antinomianism—thinking and acting as if we have a license to sin, knowing that we will be forgiven anyway. This antinomianism being shown in James is how some professing to be Christians did not love others as themselves. James is demonstrating that works are not needed for salvation, but they are proof that you are saved.

---

26 "Bible Commentary Critical and Explanatory; Jamieson, Fausset, Brown," Bible Study Tools, accessed October 18, 2018, https://www.biblestudytools.com/commentaries/jamieson-fausset-brown.

Lastly, do we need to speak in tongues as evidence of being saved? No. Speaking in tongues was a gift used to build up and encourage the church. Nowhere is it taught in the Bible that it is needed for proof of salvation.

The answer to all the questions in the title of this section is "No!" Faith alone (*sola fide*) in Christ alone (*solo Christo*) is the response to the effectual call of the Gospel. Regeneration of the heart leads to faith, which leads to repentance, which will lead to good works. Every bit of our salvation is a gift from God. There is absolutely nothing we can do to earn it. And there is nothing we can do to lose it—a controversial subject that we'll talk about next.

Chapter 8

THE MULTI-TASKER

Just as we need to have a foundational understanding of Who God the Father and Jesus the Son are, we need to also understand Who the Holy Spirit is and how He functions within the Trinity. The Holy Spirit is the third Person of the Trinity. He is first mentioned in **Genesis 1:2**: "The earth was without form and void, and darkness was over the face of the deep. And the Spirit of God was hovering over the face of the waters." The Holy Spirit is responsible for many different works in the life of a believer—some of which we've mentioned already—and we will take a further look at His work in this chapter.

THE WORK OF THE HOLY SPIRIT

In addition to the Holy Spirit's work in Creation, in the Old Testament, He gave revelation to the prophets, as we see in **Micah 3:8**: "But as for me, I am filled with power, with the Spirit of the LORD, and with justice and might, to declare to Jacob his transgression and to Israel his sin." He also enabled people to serve God: "See, I have called by name Bezalel the son of Uri, son of Hur, of the tribe of Judah, and I have filled him with the Spirit of God, with ability and intelligence, with knowledge and all craftsmanship" (**Exod. 31:2-3**).

It is important to understand that the Holy Spirit regenerated the hearts of believers in Old Testament times. They were dead in their sin—just as we are—therefore, He had to. He also empowered them for holy living then, as He does now (**Ezek. 36:26-27**). However, the Holy Spirit did not always reside in someone forever. At that time, the third Person of the Trinity sometimes came and went. "Saul was afraid of David because the LORD was with him but had departed from Saul" (**1 Sam. 18:12**). But now, Jesus promised that when He left, He would send the Holy Spirit to reside forever in a believer. "And I will ask the Father, and he will give you another Helper, to be with you forever" (**John 14:16**). We can press forward, regardless of our circumstances, and persevere here on Earth, knowing we are not alone and that we do not do anything in our own strength.

Although the Old Testament has a lot to say about the Holy Spirit, it is not made perfectly clear that the Spirit is a distinct Divine Person. It is not until the New Testament that it is clear the Spirit is distinct from the Father and from the Son. This becomes apparent when Jesus promises "another Helper." It is made clear the Holy Spirit is a personal Being from the fact that He speaks, teaches, searches, witnesses, determines, can be lied to, and can be grieved.

The Divinity of the Holy Spirit is seen in **Acts 5:3-4**: "But Peter said, 'Ananias, why has Satan filled your heart to lie to the Holy Spirit and to keep back for yourself part of the proceeds of the land? While it remained unsold, did it not remain your own? And after it was sold, was it not at your disposal? Why is it that you have contrived this deed in your heart? You have not lied to man but to God.'" His Divinity is also seen in **2 Corinthians 13:14, Revelation 1:4-6, and Matthew 28:19**. Because of His Divinity, we always refer to the Holy Spirit as "He," and not "It."

One of the things the Holy Spirit does in the life of the believer is to give them an inward witness to believe that the Bible is the Word of God! Scripture is authenticated to the believer and is also illuminated to the believer by the Holy Spirit. In **1 John 2:20**, we are told, "But you have been anointed by the Holy One, and you all have knowledge." Likewise, **2 Corinthians 4:6** says, "For God, who said, 'Let light shine out of darkness,' has shone in our hearts to give the light of the knowledge of the glory of God in the face of Jesus Christ." The light mentioned in this verse is the same word used in the Septuagint (the Greek version of the Hebrew Bible) in **Psalm 44:3**—"the light of your face"—and in **Psalm 78:14**—"In the daytime he led them with a cloud, and all the night with a fiery light." The Holy Spirit shines the light on Scripture, making the believer's heart know that it is, indeed, God's Word. He illuminates our hearts to help us understand it and helps us discern truth from false teaching.

As we saw in chapter four, part of the work of the Holy Spirit is to regenerate the hearts of the elect so that they can respond to the Gospel message. It's important, for the sake of understanding, to note that regeneration, responding to the Gospel in faith, and being justified can be something that happens at once. However, we need to know how they fall in order—not from the standpoint of time progression, but the sequence in which they logically go. Once God has declared us righteous (justified), we're adopted! We have access to God the Father, through Jesus Christ! (FYI: That is why we pray to God the Father in the name of Jesus Christ).

So, what happens after that? Sanctification. This is oftentimes a painful process, but one that feels more and more right, as you come through each painful lesson, even when those lessons need to be repeated several times. How can something feel so bad, and yet so right at the same time? The process of being more and more conformed to God's will is transforming you to the way you were meant to be—like our first parents before the Fall.

Sanctification is our increasing in the knowledge of Jesus and conforming to His image. This also is a work of God, done by the Holy Spirit with our cooperation in God's timing. Sanctification is not something that happens to you all at once; it's a lifelong process here on Earth. You (and me) will never be completely like Jesus until we are finally with Him, either through death or His second coming! But for now, more and more, you will die to sin and live for righteousness.

When we accept Jesus as our Savior, we are "born again" into a new spiritual life. The "old man" (the old way of our thinking) dies, and the new man (with new thinking having the ability to love God and not sin) is born. At that same time, the Holy Spirit comes to live inside of us. Jesus told His apostles that He was leaving after His resurrection. He said that His leaving would actually be better for those who are His. "Nevertheless, I tell you the truth: It is to your advantage that I go away, for if I do not go away, the Helper will not come to you. But if I go, I will send him to you" (**John 16:7**). Jesus said this because upon His leaving, He would send a Comforter. Someone Who will not only bring you comfort, but Who Jesus says, "will teach you all things and bring to your remembrance all that I have said to you" (**John 14:26**). In other words, He will help us remember things we've learned about God when we need it.

The Holy Spirit will also be our Counselor to guide us in our everyday lives. This includes convicting us of our sin, even sin we aren't aware of. He will also help us to stop sinning and to do things that please God! And He will help us to pray—even when we are not sure what to pray for ourselves. When we are without words in prayer, He is not! He is also called *Paraclete*, from the Greek word meaning "one who gives support."[27] He supports us by being our Helper, Adviser, Ally, Encourager, and Strengthener, along with all the other things we've mentioned! Talk about multi-tasking!

The Holy Spirit is also our Seal for eternity in Heaven, as we are told in Ephesians 1:13: "In him you also, when you heard the word of truth, the gospel of your salvation, and believed in him, were sealed with the promised Holy Spirit." With that being said, if the Holy Spirit is living inside us and is our forever Seal from the moment we become a Christian, is it possible to lose Him and/or salvation?

---

27 J.I. Packer.

SAVED, SEALED, DELIVERED, WE'RE HIS!

As we said at the end of the chapter seven, the issue of whether or not you can lose your salvation is a controversial one, and it's one that's been argued for a long time. Certainly, there are some verses in Scripture that, taken by themselves, make it sound like you can lose your salvation. But when the verses are put into context, that notion is negated. We're going to take a look at some of these Scriptures.

So, what happens as we walk through this life, becoming more and more like Jesus, but at the same time still having difficulties and hardships and still being sinners? Although we will still sin, sometimes grievously, we can never lose our salvation. This is referred to as the "Perseverance of the Saints." Contrary to what some believe, it is not called that because we persist under hardship and discouragement. It would be better understood as *Jesus, through the Holy Spirit, preserving us.* Our perseverance is not up to us; it is up to God because of His immutability (unchangeability) of His decree of election.

"Saved" is a permanent status. In **John 10:25-30**, Jesus tells the unbelieving Jews who were there that they did not believe "because [they were] not among my sheep." His sheep hear His voice and follow Him. He also tells them that His Father gave them to Him, and that no one can snatch them out of His hand! This is echoed in **John 17:2-11**. And **John 6:37-39** reiterates, "All that the Father gives me will come to me, and whoever comes to me I will never cast out. For I have come down from heaven, not to do my own will but to do the will of him who sent me, that I should lose nothing of all that he has given me, but raise it up at the last day." If you are a believer, God the Father gave you to Jesus, and He will never lose you! We can have assurance of our faith always, even when it feels like God is not near.

Some people believe the Bible says that we can lose our salvation. The fight over this question really begins with one thing: What state do you believe the human race has been in since Adam and Eve sinned? This may seem like a strange question to start with when talking about the assurance of your salvation, but it really is the key to many of the questions surrounding how sure we can be that "saved" is a forever state.

Many people who consider themselves evangelical Christians today believe that salvation is by man's own choice or based on his own moral character. These beliefs usually fall into one of three categories, or sometimes a mixture of the following:

1. One belief is that Adam's sin did not affect all of humanity; therefore, human beings are born innocent, and it is the freedom of the human will to choose either good or evil. This is known as Pelagianism. This idea has been condemned by several church councils, and Pelagius was condemned as a heretic and excommunicated in 418 AD. And rightly so. **Romans 5:12** (as well as many other verses) tells us something different: "Therefore, just as sin came into the world through one man, and death through sin, and so death spread to all men because all sinned."

2. Another view believes every person is depraved, but not totally. This view is called Arminianism. This view believes that everyone has a "little bit" of good left in them, that people were only "weakened" by the Fall and not spiritually deadened. It's the belief that the Fall left mankind only sick and in need of an antibiotic, instead of dead and in need of the paddles to restart our cold, stony, dead hearts. The belief is that in this state, man is still "good enough" to be able to reach out to God, to respond to His "wooing," to muster-up faith in response to the Gospel message. The idea is that man makes the first move—he reaches out to God first; then God gives him grace.

3. A view similar but different than number two is the belief that human beings were deadened by the fall of Adam, but that God gave

everyone a "little island of grace" (which is known as "Prevenient Grace"). This view is called Wesleyanism. This small amount of grace begins the process of drawing a person to God. It prepares the heart for hearing the Gospel, but it can be resisted. Prevenient grace is universal, meaning all humans receive it, regardless of their having heard of Jesus.

In chapter three, we looked at many parts of Scripture that tell us man is totally dead in his sin, hostile to God, having no inclination to seek God. Since man is dead, he cannot initiate any part of salvation. A dead man in a casket cannot possibly reach out his hand for help. He's dead! His only hope is for someone to bring him back to life by restarting his heart. Who is the only One who can accomplish this? It's God.

Keep in mind, we are talking about this in regard to whether or not our salvation can be lost. This is why it's important to go back to Who initiates salvation—whether man does, or God does. The Pelagianism described in view number one is humanism or moralism, not Christianity, so we won't go any further in discussing it, except to say that we should watch out for churches and preachers who tend to focus on our moral behavior, instead of Christ's righteousness imputed to us.

In views two and three, the belief is that fallen man has enough righteousness in him (by either means), that he might actually seek God and have a desire to reach out to God for salvation. With this belief, the next logical thought is that you make the decision (based on your human free will) to accept or believe in Jesus when you hear the Gospel message. This would make it a meritorious earning of salvation because you would have done some part of it (making the right choice) to earn your own salvation. Luther's Ninety-five Theses nailed to the door of the church in Wittenberg (the "start" of the Protestant Reformation) was in response to the Catholic church's selling indulgences, which were touted to lessen the punishment for sins. There's much more to it than that, but the bottom line is that you cannot pay for sins yourself. Not in any way. Luther was against the idea of someone being led to believe that anything other than Christ's death on the cross could pay for sins, and we should be against that idea, too!

If your salvation is your choice to make (or not), then your choosing constitutes your having to do something to earn it. This is merit-based, works-based theology. If this is what you believe, while you may say with your mouth that Christ is the One Who saved you, you will see, if you think it through logically, that what you really believe is that Christ has already done His part, BUT you still have to do YOUR part by choosing correctly. That's not grace. God's grace in salvation is "unmerited favor."[28]

Think of it this way. When you stand before God, what will you bring in your hands to offer for salvation? Are you bringing nothing, relying totally on the merit of what Jesus did for you? Or are you offering God what Jesus did on the cross, plus your "correct decision"?

Our sinful nature wants us to be "totally free" to make our own choices and rule our own lives. It naturally fights the idea of a totally sovereign God working out His plans. The term "free will" gets tossed around a lot in Christian circles, but the truth is, this idea is used in the Bible in terms of offerings, gifts, and other things; but it is not used in regard to choosing our salvation at all. Think about it—if we had to choose God (if we had the ability to), do you really picture God, the Creator of the universe, hoping, wishing, maybe even wringing His hands, while He waits to see if we accept Him or not? On another note, if everyone universally was given an "island of righteousness," regardless of whether they ever hear about Jesus or not, wouldn't that constitute God actually "choosing" (at least some) by way of who gets to hear the Gospel and who doesn't?

The idea that we contribute something is seductive. Because of our sinful nature, we want desperately to stand on our own two feet. We do not like the

---

28 *The New Strong's Exhaustive Concordance*, s.v. "Grace," Nashville, TN: Thomas Nelson Publishers, 1965.

idea of needing help, let alone the idea of being totally helpless before anyone, even God! However, leaning on our own righteousness, to any degree, leaves us with many questions that need to be answered. Questions that can crush a believer's faith, leave him with anxiety, or leave him with no surety of salvation. This is how much of the evangelical Christian community lives today! If we are taught that our salvation is partially up to us, in any way, we will wonder if we've done enough, done it correctly, were sincere enough, if we know enough. We will be plagued with wondering whether we've actually done what is required in order to "close the deal."

The biblical reality is that God elects all those who are His before the foundation of the world. And then He brings them to a saving knowledge of Him. This is what Scripture teaches the whole way through the Book—from Abraham, to Lydia, to Paul, and on and on, and to you and to me. Even David's kindnesses to Mephibosheth is a picture of God's grace to us.

If you've never heard this before and are having trouble believing it, read through the Bible from start to finish, and find someone—anyone—who went searching after God in order to be saved! You won't find it. Abraham was living in the Ur of the Chaldeans and was part of a pagan-worshiping family. Mephibosheth never sought out David; David sought him out. Lydia's eyes were opened by God before she heard the Gospel. Paul could not have been farther from believing the Gospel when God opened his eyes. Up until then, he was killing Christians! The bottom line is, we are never inclined to go after God in our fallen state. We can't. He has to reach out to us by regenerating our hearts.

When we have had our hearts regenerated by the Holy Spirit, we definitely will, at some point, accept the Gospel message and be born again. This rebirth is monergistic (*ergo* meaning "work/exertion"; *mono* meaning "one").[29] Salvation is the work of One—not One, plus your work. It is not the work of two; it is not synergistic. Salvation is of God alone—from start to finish.

---

29 Theopedia, *s.v. "monergistic,"* accessed December 9, 2018, https://www.theopedia.com/monergism.

Why does your view of man's state since the Fall—whether man is dead or just sick, totally depraved, or having an "island of righteousness"—make a difference in whether or not you believe salvation can be lost? If you believe that man is responsible for any part of his own salvation, then the logical conclusion is that 1) it's man's option to walk away from his salvation and 2) that he may not ever have done enough to actually secure it. In other words, he may have missed the mark!

But if God's electing love is what you believe saved you, then it's logical to believe that He absolutely will continue to do so. If God has done all of the saving, from start to finish, why wouldn't He bring it to completion? What would be the point if He didn't? And we would say a hearty AMEN to that! **Philippians 1:6** says, "And I am sure of this, that he who began a good work in you will bring it to completion at the day of Jesus Christ."

WARNINGS AGAINST FALLING AWAY

In spite of all that we've just covered, there are several Scripture references that seem to say that we can lose our salvation. Here's a brief look at some of them, and what is really going on in each passage:

- **Romans 11**—At the beginning of this chapter, Paul is asked if God has rejected His people, Israel. Paul's Jewish heritage was evidence that God had not fully rejected Israel. Paul goes on to explain that God, in His electing love, had formed a remnant to be saved, by grace and not by works. He then talks about Israel being "broken off" and Gentiles "grafted in" to provoke the jealousy of the Jews unto salvation. (God uses many means to bring His elect remnant to salvation.) There are warnings to the Gentiles not to boast because salvation is totally based on grace. This passage is about God's elect remnant to be saved, including both Jewish and Gentile believers.

- **Galatians 5:4**—"You are severed from Christ, you who would be justified by the law; you have fallen away from grace." In this passage, Paul is admonishing believers for relying on the law (circumcision) instead of relying solely on Christ. This is an admonishment against works-based salvation. Just as Luther said, this is a "return to Rome." Remember, a Christian rests in faith alone, in Christ alone. He adds nothing to save himself.

- **Colossians 1:21-23**—"And you, who once were alienated and hostile in mind, doing evil deeds, he has now reconciled in his body of flesh by his death, in order to present you holy and blameless and above reproach before him, if indeed you continue in the faith, stable and steadfast, not shifting from the hope of the gospel that you heard . . . " Paul again admonishes believers for coming under false teaching from Judaism and Greek philosophy, which was causing them to try to placate other "spiritual forces." True believers cannot worship other gods while also claiming to be Christian. Adding other religious practices to Christianity is never okay. This is called syncretism, and it is what the Israelites were consistently doing in the Old Testament—adding false religions to Judaism. Christians rely solely on the finished work of Christ.

- **James 5:19-20**—"My brothers, if anyone among you wanders from the truth and someone brings him back, let him know that whoever brings back a sinner from his wandering will save his soul from death and will cover a multitude of sins." This passage is talking about praying for each other (Jas. 5:15) in regard to "righting" someone who is a believer, who is falling into sinful patterns of behavior, which may be evidence of the absence of saving faith. It is an admonishment to the body that we should look out for one another.

- **2 Peter 2:20-22**—"For if, after they have escaped the defilements of the world through the knowledge of our Lord and Savior Jesus Christ, they are again entangled in them and overcome, the last state has become worse for them that at the first. For it would have been better for them never to have known the way of righteousness than after knowing it to turn back from the holy commandment delivered to them. What the true proverb says has happened to them: 'The dog returns to its own vomit and, the sow, after washing herself, returns to wallow in the mire.'" This passage is about false teachers, who had been part of the visible church, claiming to be Christians, but who are, in reality, apostate—those who have claimed to be a Christian, but later renounce it. Apostates have never had a true heart change and, therefore, were never a true believer to begin with.

GOATS AMONG SHEEP

Jesus is coming back again. When He does, He will separate out the unbelievers (goats) from the elect/believers (sheep). **Matthew 25:31-46** is a clear picture of Jesus doing this:

> When the Son of Man comes in his glory, and all the angels with him, then he will sit on his glorious throne. Before him will be gathered all the nations, and he will separate people one from another as a shepherd separates the sheep from the goats. And he will place the sheep on his right, but the goats on his left . . . Then the King will say to those on his right, "Come, you who are blessed by my Father, inherit the kingdom prepared for you from the foundation of the world . . . " Then he will say to those on his left, "Depart from me, you cursed, into the eternal fire prepared for the devil and his angels . . . " And these will go away into eternal punishment, but the righteous into eternal life.

Right now, we attend worship services as a mixed group of sheep and goats. Not everyone who goes to church is really saved. These "goats" may experience blessings from God because of their close association with the faithful; but in the end, they will suffer eternal judgment. In **Matthew 7:21**, Jesus says, "Not everyone who says to me, 'Lord, Lord,' will enter the kingdom of heaven, but the one who does the will of my Father who is in heaven." There are even many who will speak and act no different from a true believer. God is not fooled. "This people . . . honor me with their lips, while their hearts are far from me" (**Isa. 29:13**). This truth is reiterated in **Matthew 15:8** and **Mark 7:6**.

Augustine pointed out that the visible church consists of both the "wheat" and the "tares" with an invisible distinction:

> O you Christians, whose lives are good, you sigh and groan as being few among many, few among very many. The winter will pass away, the summer will come; lo! The harvest will soon be here. The angels will come who can make the separation, and who cannot make mistakes . . . I tell you of a truth, my Beloved, even in these high seats there is both wheat, and tares, and among the laity there is wheat, and tares.[30]

If you have a genuine faith, you will never lose it; if you lose it, you never had it. Those who recant their faith never had it. This is the example from **1 John 2:19**: "They went out from us, but they were not of us; for if they had been of us, they would have continued with us. But they went out, that it might become plain that they all are not of us." This was not an instance where people in the church lost their salvation; these people were never saved in the first place.

Hebrew 6:1-12 also has warnings for those who may be in church, but are not believers. This passage comes on the heels of a warning about having knowledge that is only superficial. True believers will desire to gain a deeper

---

30 Philip Schaff, ed., *The Nicene and Post-Nicene Fathers, First Series,* Vol. 108, Grand Rapids, MI: Eerdmans, 1979.

knowledge of the Bible. They won't be happy with "milk"; they will crave solid food. Then comes the warning to those who've "been enlightened." This would be someone who's familiar with knowledge of God and the Gospel, maybe even someone who's used their gifts and talents for God or the church, but never comes to a true, saving knowledge of Christ. It's talking even more so about the flagrant sin of one who falls in this category. The clearest example of someone in that situation would be Judas Iscariot. Apostates generally appear to be genuine believers. But they never were.

It's important to say here that sometimes truly regenerate believers backslide and fall into gross sin. Usually they make themselves (and most likely others) miserable, but their miserable state will eventually lead them to seek and find restoration to righteousness.

Because continuing in the faith is dependent on God and not us, Christians will still sin, sometimes even seriously, backsliding in ways that we can't believe! Many Christians see this; and their first reaction is to say the person has lost their salvation. The truth is, none of us know what sins we are still capable of doing, even after years or decades of being a Christian. The prime example of this is David, who committed adultery and murder. David sinned grievously but was still called "a man after God's own heart." He may have fallen away from grace, but he never fell out of grace. However, it took the prophet Nathan confronting him about his sin before he repented of it.

The second example is Peter. Peter denied Jesus—the same thing Judas did. Peter made a public denial of Jesus, even though Jesus had warned him beforehand that he was going to do it. The difference between Judas and Peter is that Peter was one of Jesus' own. We know that because Jesus tells Peter that He has prayed for him; and while Peter was repentant of what he did, Judas only felt guilt about what he did.

Christians can have radical, serious falls, but they are not total and final falls from grace. And we should never have a puffed-up view of our own selves, lest we fall. We do not know what's in a person's heart. Only God knows that. Church discipline, even to the point of excommunication, is for the purpose of bringing a believer to repentance. It helps maintain the purity of the church and the restoration of a believer to his usefulness in the body of Christ. We see this with the case of the incestuous man in **2 Corinthians**. In that chapter, Paul admonishes them to bring him back into the fold. "For such a one, this punishment by the majority is enough, so you should rather turn to forgive and comfort him, or he may be overwhelmed by excessive sorrow. So I beg you to reaffirm your love for him" (verses six through eight). There is no reason we should think that we should do otherwise. Our example is Christ, and He welcomed Peter back! Therefore, if someone turns and comes back, we are called to be forbearing and to "cover a multitude of sins" (**1 Peter 4:8**).

Being in a local church body is important for the Christian's perseverance. In *Pilgrim's Progress* by John Bunyan, we have an allegory in which Christian (the pilgrim) meets up with others along his journey. Christian meets a list of bad characters, as well as good ones who encourage him along the way and who spur him toward righteousness as he goes. Each one has different gifts that help and equip him—each named accordingly (Charity, Discretion, Piety, Faithful, Hopeful, etc.). We need other believers in our lives to equip and help us, too. We need admonishment; we need encouragement; we need faithful friends who will listen. **First Peter 1:1** tells us that we are, by nature, "elect exiles" here on Earth. This is not our home. We are strangers, foreigners in a strange land, and we need God's other peculiar people in our lives to help us on our journey.

PERSEVERANCE OR PRESERVATION?

Again, the theological point we have been talking about is "the Perseverance of the Saints." As we said, it is more accurate to think of it as "God's preserving us," then "us persevering." Reformers have often looked at this in light of both definitions. Reformed theologians generally understand the perseverance of the saints as God's preservation of believers, while also recognizing the believer's responsibility at persevering in their faith, even through hardship. It's a realization that believers persist under discouragement and pressure and are able to do so because Jesus Christ through the Holy Spirit ensures that we will endure to the end. It affirms that true faith is accompanied by action or else it is dead. "So also faith by itself, if it does not have works, is dead" (**James 2:17**). Paul tells the Philippian church "work out your own salvation with fear and trembling" in **Philippians 2:12**. He also says that a Christian's life and faith are tested to see whether the person is truly saved. "Examine yourselves, to see whether you are in the faith; Test yourselves. Or do you not realize this about yourselves, that Jesus Christ is in you?—unless indeed you fail to meet the test" (**2 Cor. 13:5**). In this way, reformed theologians often distinguish saving faith from a seemingly sincere, but temporary, faith shown by hypocrisy and apostasy.

Nevertheless, reformed theology also emphasizes God's gracious preservation to sustain true believers. Christians go through life in continual reliance on Christ. Paul exhorted the Philippians to work out their salvation, but at the end added, "For it is God who works in you, both to will and to work for his good pleasure" (**Phil. 2:13**). Paul also tells us that "he who began a good work in you will bring it to completion" (**Phil. 1:6**). And **Hebrews 7:25** says, "He is able to save to the uttermost those who draw near to God through him, since he always lives to make intercession for them." These, along with previously stated texts and others, affirm these truths.

Having Jesus as our great High Priest is another reason to be confident that our salvation is forever. Like it says in this verse in Hebrews, Jesus is in Heaven right now interceding for us daily, as we've said before in this book. He is praying for His people. Judas and Peter both betrayed Jesus. But like we already said, Jesus never prayed for Judas; He told Judas to "do quickly" what he was going to do (**John 13:27**). God had a purpose for Judas, but he was never one of Jesus' sheep. Judas was called the "Son of Perdition" from the beginning. On the other hand, Jesus prayed for Peter because he was one of Jesus' own. Jesus prayed for him and also told him, "Simon, Simon, behold, Satan demanded to have you, that he might sift you like wheat, but I have prayed for you that your faith may not fail. And when you have turned again, strengthen your brothers" (**Luke 22:31**). Two public deniers of Jesus, two different outcomes.

It is the Holy Spirit Who raises us to eternal life. God starts with a promise to finish. The Holy Spirit helps with our preservation. We are sealed, and we are given the Spirit as a down-payment of our salvation. While people may put a down-payment on something and then walk away from it, God never does. Since it is God putting the down-payment on His elect, He is going to preserve those whose names are in the Book of Life the whole way through this life.

COMFORT, COMFORT, YE MY PEOPLE

The doctrine of the Perseverance of the Saints is a comfort to saints who are struggling with sin. It is a comfort to the dying, to those who need encouragement, to parents of prodigals; and it's comforting to every believer. It takes away the questions of whether we've done enough, done it correctly, were sincere enough, or know enough. We don't have to "close the deal." In fact, we never could!

If you are a believer in Christ, nothing can separate you from the love of God. You were chosen before the foundation of the world, bought with the precious blood of Christ, sealed with the Holy Spirit, and will be a citizen of Heaven someday. Christian, you really can take comfort in the assurance of your salvation. The Bible tells us so. We end with these words from Paul in **Romans 8:34-39**:

> Who is to condemn? Christ Jesus is the one who died—more than that, who was raised—who is at the right hand of God, who

indeed is interceding for us. Who shall separate us from the love of Christ? Shall tribulation, or distress, or persecution, or famine, or nakedness, or danger, or sword? As it is written: "For your sake we are being killed all the day long; we are regarded as sheep to be slaughtered." No, in all these things we are more than conquerors through him who loved us. For I am sure that neither death nor life, nor angels nor rulers, nor things present nor things to come, nor powers, nor height nor depth, nor anything else in all creation, will be able to separate us from the love of God in Christ Jesus our Lord.

Chapter 9

PRICELESS REWARDS AND ROYAL RESPONSIBILITIES

Besides assurance of eternal salvation and the gift of the Holy Spirit, there are other rewards that come with being a child of God! There are also responsibilities.

When we respond to the Gospel in faith, we are adopted into God's family. **Romans 8:16-17** tells us, "The Spirit himself bears witness with our spirit that we are children of God, and if children, then heirs—heirs of God and fellow heirs with Christ, provided we suffer with him in order that we may also be glorified with him." This means that we are heirs of our Father's Kingdom, a subject explored in the following chapter. It also means that since we are in Christ, we can have access to the Father. And we have an inheritance. The rich young ruler wanted to know what he had to *do* to inherit eternal life within God's Kingdom. However, inheritance isn't based on what we *do*; it's based on being part of the family.

We're also told in **Romans 8:29**, "For those whom he (God) foreknew he also predestined to be conformed to the image of his Son, in order that he might be the firstborn among many brothers." So if you are an only child, you won't be anymore!

As if all of that weren't enough, once Jesus becomes our Lord and Savior, we also receive inclusion into the Kingdom of God! Just as salvation cannot be lost, once we have citizenship into the Kingdom of God, it, too, can never be lost! As **Daniel 7:18** tells us, "But the saints of the Most High shall receive the kingdom and possess the kingdom forever, forever and ever."

WHAT EXACTLY IS THE KINGDOM OF GOD?

The Hebrew word for kingdom is *malkut*, and the Greek word is *basileia*. Both terms primarily mean "rule" or "reign," and both terms refer to the exercise of God's power, dominion, or sovereignty. **Psalm 103:19** illustrates this: "The Lord has established his throne in the heavens, and his kingdom rules over all."

The Kingdom of God is mentioned 126 times in the Gospels and a total of 160 times throughout the New Testament.[31] Most of these references come directly from Jesus. Sometimes, the Kingdom of God is referred to as the Kingdom of Heaven. It was once thought by some that the Kingdom of God and the Kingdom of Heaven were two different realities. Now, however, it is clearly understood that they are one and the same. This is evident for several reasons. For one, the two expressions are used in the same sayings of Jesus by different Gospel writers. Usually, it is Matthew who uses "kingdom of heaven," and Mark or Luke who use "kingdom of God." An example of this is found in **Matthew 5:3**: "Blessed are the poor in spirit, for theirs is the kingdom of heaven." Another example is **Luke 6:20**: "Blessed are you who are poor, for yours is the kingdom of God."

Second, Matthew also uses "Kingdom of God." He uses the two expressions interchangeably in **Matthew 19:23-24**: "Truly, I say to you, only with difficulty will a rich person enter the kingdom of heaven. Again I tell you, it is easier for a camel to go through the eye of a needle than for a rich person to enter the kingdom of God."

---

31 John Piper, "What Is the Kingdom of God?" DesiringGod.org, accessed October 17, 2018, https://www.desiringgod.org/interviews/what-is-the-kingdom-of-god.

Finally, the word "heaven" was frequently used as a substitutionary word for God by devout Jews due to the third commandment: "You shall not take the name of the LORD your God in vain (Exod. 20:7). They wanted to be sure not to use the Lord's name in vain by mistake, so to be safe, they just used the word "heaven" instead. This makes sense as to why it is usually Matthew who uses "kingdom of heaven." Matthew was writing his Gospel to the Jewish people.

The Kingdom of God was part of the central message of Jesus. Throughout the Gospels, we see the theme of "Repent, for the kingdom of heaven is at hand" repeated.[32] Also, every one of the forty-six different parables Jesus told was about the Kingdom of God.

Okay, we clearly get that the Kingdom of God is paramount. But what exactly is it? There is no one-line definition for the Kingdom of God. It is somewhat mysterious and complex.

1. **The Kingdom of God has always been.** The Kingdom of God is not a geographical place like the United Kingdom or the Kingdom of Saudi Arabia. Instead, it is God's Sovereign reign over His people. More precisely, it is **God's Redemptive Reign. Isaiah 37:16** says, "You are the God, you alone of all the kingdoms of the earth; you have made heaven and earth." This verse, and several others, shows us that the Kingdom of God is not a place, but the redemptive rule, reign, and sovereignty of God. God has always reigned and is sovereign over everything and everyone in the entire universe.

   His "redemptive" reign is His reign over His people (the ones He has chosen to save through Jesus). Since He chose His people before the creation of the world, He has always had a redemptive reign on them; this means the Kingdom of God existed before the foundation of the world. **Ephesians 1:4-5** illustrates this beautifully: "Even as he chose us in him before the foundation of the world, that we

---

32   Matthew 3:2; Matthew 4:17; Mark 1:15.

should be holy and blameless before him. In love he predestined us for adoption to himself as sons through Jesus Christ, according to the purpose of his will."

What being a part of His redemptive reign means for us is spelled out in **Colossians 1:13-14**: "He has delivered us from the domain of darkness and transferred us to the kingdom of his beloved Son, in whom we have redemption, the forgiveness of sins." Charles Spurgeon says this about this verse in Colossians: "Beloved we still are tempted by Satan, but we are not under his power; we have to fight with him, but we are not his slaves. He is not our king; he has no rights over us; we do not obey him; we will not listen to his temptations."[33]

Throughout history, when people are overthrown by a kingdom or government—such as the kingdom of Judah being overthrown by Babylon or the United States overthrowing the Kingdom of Hawaii—the pattern is the same. The conquered people belong to their captors and must adhere to the laws and regulations of their new sovereignty. When we are "overthrown" by the Kingdom of God upon our salvation, we now belong to God and come under His reign.

2. **The Kingdom of God is now**. From **Matthew 3**, we see that John the Baptist's mission was to prepare the people for the coming of God's Kingdom on Earth. How was it coming? Through the Messiah, Jesus. When that little Baby was born in Bethlehem, it was the beginning of the fulfillment of God's redemptive reign on His people. But Jesus didn't just usher in the Kingdom of God; He *is* the Kingdom of God. He is both the King and the Kingdom! **Matthew 12:28** shows us that Jesus is *the King* of the Kingdom: "But if it is by the Spirit of God that I cast out demons, then the kingdom of God has come upon you." **Luke 17:21** shows us that Jesus *is* the Kingdom: "The kingdom of God

---

[33] Charles Haddon Spurgeon, *Sermons of Rev. C.H. Spurgeon of London*, S.l.: Forgotten Books, 2015.

is in the midst of you." Jesus established God's Kingdom on Earth by triumphing over sin, Satan, and death. He proclaims this Kingdom to the elect, granting them admission into it and deploying them to further it. When we trust in the work Christ did, we gain citizenship into the Kingdom of God, thereby relinquishing our citizenship of this world.

3. **The Kingdom of God has yet to come**. When we pray the Lord's prayer as Jesus taught us in **Matthew 6:5-15** and **Luke 11:1-13**, we say, "Your kingdom come." This would imply that the Kingdom of God has not yet come. How can that be when the Kingdom of God is God's redemptive reign—which has always been—and Jesus—Who is now? We did warn you the Kingdom of God was mysterious! It has always been because God has always been Sovereign, and it is now because Jesus ushered it in; but there is a part of the Kingdom that is still yet to come.

If we finish the line from the Lord's prayer—"Your kingdom come . . . on earth as it is in heaven" (Matt. 6:10)—we get the answer. God's Kingdom will be complete when Heaven is established on Earth. In other words, when Jesus comes back.

One Christian commentary said this:

> It is important to realize that for the New Testament authors, the coming of the kingdom, or reign of God, does not occur at a single moment in time. Instead, the coming of the kingdom involves a series of events that occur over a period of time. When Jesus declares that the kingdom of God has come and yet that it is coming, He is saying that the prophesied last act in the drama of redemption has begun but that it has not yet reached its conclusion. In other words, Jesus is saying that we are now in the midst of the last act.[34]

---

34 Keith Mathison, "Thy Kingdom Come by Keith Mathison," Ligonier Ministries, accessed October 17, 2018, https://www.ligonier.org/learn/articles/thy-kingdom-come/.

When we pray "Your kingdom come, your will be done, on earth as it is in heaven," we are praying that things on Earth will be as they are in Heaven: All hearts are following Jesus; all mouths are proclaiming Jesus is Lord; God's enemies are a footstool beneath His feet; and Satan, evil, sin, and rebellion against God are eternally punished. This is what the coming Kingdom of God will look like—the Kingdom that will arrive when Jesus returns.

Matthew 13:41-43 gives us a glimpse into the kingdom to come: "The Son of Man will send his angels, and they will gather out of his kingdom all causes of sin and all law-breakers, and throw them into the fiery furnace. In that place there will be weeping and gnashing of teeth. Then the righteous will shine like the sun in the kingdom of their Father." **Revelation 21:1-4** completes the picture further:

> Then I saw a new heaven and a new earth, for the first heaven and the first earth had passed away, and the sea was no more. And I saw the holy city, new Jerusalem, coming down out of heaven from God, prepared as a bride adorned for her husband. And I heard a loud voice from the throne saying, "Behold, the dwelling place of God is with man. He will dwell with them, and they will be his people, and God himself will be with them as their God. He will wipe every tear from their eyes, and *death* shall be no more, neither shall there be mourning, nor crying, nor pain anymore, for the former things have passed away."

ROYAL RESPONSIBILITIES

As a citizen of the Kingdom, we are called to live the life of the Kingdom. As **1 Peter 2:9** tells us, "But you are a chosen race, a royal priesthood, a holy nation, a people for his own possession, that you may proclaim the excellencies of him who called you out of darkness into his wonderful light."

When we are adopted into the family of God and into the Kingdom of God, we are a child of the King. That makes us princes and princesses! Ask any royal, and they will tell you that the title comes with responsibility. For us, one responsibility is knowing we are owned by God, purchased by the blood of Jesus, and that we owe ourselves as a living sacrifice to God. What does that mean? We were dead. God could have left us in that state, but He chose to raise us from the dead to new life. Now that we are alive in Christ, we need to shed our old, "dead" self. The dead has no place with the living. We also have an obligation to Jesus as the One Who resurrected us and brought us to life! Charles Spurgeon says, "It is a test of our claim to be Christians. Does anger have dominion over you? Does murmuring and complaining? Does covetousness have dominion over you? Does pride? Does laziness have dominion over you? If sin has dominion over us, we should serious [sic] ask if we are really converted."[35]

Another responsibility of being royalty in the Kingdom of God is that we are to be His witness. **Luke 24:45-48** tells us, "Then he [Jesus] opened their minds to understand the Scriptures, and said to them, 'Thus it is written, That the Christ should suffer and on the third day rise from the dead, and that repentance for the forgiveness of sins should be proclaimed in his name to all nations, beginning from Jerusalem. You are witnesses of these things.'" Once the Holy Spirit opens our minds to understand the Gospel, Jesus commands us to go tell others!

I heard of a Chinese farmer who had cataracts removed from his eyes at a Christian mission clinic. A few days later, the missionary doctor looked out his window and noticed this farmer holding the end of a long rope. Holding onto the rope in a single file were several dozen blind Chinese who had been rounded up and led for miles to the doctor who had worked a miracle on this farmer's eyes. That's how we who have received God's gift of forgiveness and eternal life through Jesus Christ should be. We have the only Physician Who

---

[35] Spurgeon.

can cure the deadly disease that ails the human race (sin). We should want to tell as many as we can about this miraculous Doctor!

Is it necessary that every Christian evangelize, even if you don't have the gift of evangelism? We can answer this by asking these questions. If you do not have the gift of mercy, does that mean you are exempt from showing mercy to people? If you do not have the gift of service, does that mean you can skate by, never doing anything for anyone else? The answer to these questions is "of course not!"—the same answer to the question regarding evangelism.

While some may be stronger in evangelism, none of us is exempt from it. Like all spiritual gifts, we are all called to use them, even if we are not strong in them. As with anything, the more you use them, the better they will be. Spiritual gifts are not something that is given once by the Holy Spirit, and that's it. They can be nurtured and developed. So, while you may not be strong in the gift of evangelism right now, with a little work and lots of practice, it could turn into your top gift somewhere down the road! Even if it doesn't, you can still grow in it and become more proficient at it.

First Corinthians 13:13 says, "So now faith, hope, and love abide . . . but the greatest of these is love." What does this love look like? Throughout Scripture, love is not the warm, fuzzy feeling you get when you love someone. Biblical love is a verb, not an adverb! Jesus says the very essence of the Law is to love God and love others (Matt. 22:36-40). He does not say it should make us tingle. He doesn't even say that we have to like a person in order to love them! Biblical love is putting the needs and interests of another person before your own. When we understand this, witnessing to people seems like the most logical and necessary thing to do.

EASY FOR YOU TO SAY

Sometimes, we hesitate to witness the Gospel message because we don't want to sound "preachy" or like "Bible-thumpers." We may fear rejection or ridicule from people. To that, Paul would say, "Poppycock!" **Romans 1:16** says, "For I am not ashamed of the gospel, for it is the power of God for salvation to everyone who believes." **This was a radical statement Paul was making!** This word *Gospel* in the original Greek is a word that was seldom used at the time this was written. Nobody talked this way because the word literally means "nearly-too-good-to-be-true news." It referred to news that was so awesome, nothing really justified using it. There was nothing that was too good to be true—that is, until Jesus came along! Which is precisely the point Paul is making.

Because what Jesus did for us is the only thing in all of history worthy of being labeled "Gospel," we cannot alter it. We cannot try to avoid feelings of shame by altering the Gospel message to make it popular and inoffensive. As **1 Corinthians 2:14** says, "The natural person does not accept the things of the Spirit of God, for they are folly to him, and he is not able to understand them because they are spiritually discerned." As this verse tells us, for those whose hearts has not been regenerated by the Holy Spirit, the Gospel will sound silly no matter how we present it; but for those whose hearts have been regenerated, it will be the life-saving message they desperately need to hear.

Since we have no idea whose hearts have been regenerated and whose haven't been, we are to have the approach that all the hearts we speak to have been regenerated. We need to speak the true, complete Gospel message to everyone, so the elect will hear the power of God! For like the true Jesus, the Gospel has the power to transform someone, and we don't want to misrepresent it. Neither Judaism, Buddhism, Hinduism, nor Islam has a Savior Who can solve the problem of separation from a holy God because of sin. Only Christianity offers sinners hope by grace alone (*sola gratia*). Misrepresenting the Gospel could make Christianity seem no different than other religions and raise the question, "What's the big deal about it then?"

We may be tempted to think, *Well, it was easy for Paul to preach the Gospel, but it's just not that easy for me.* Paul was mistrusted by the apostles, hated by the Pharisees, beaten, imprisoned, left for dead, and ultimately beheaded for the sake of the Gospel. What kept him going? In his own words, "It is the power of God for salvation to everyone who believes" (**Rom. 1:16**). For Paul, being a part of the process in bringing people to salvation was worth any cost he had to incur—even death.

We are certain to come up against opposition. One of the "consequences" of being royalty in the family of God is that you will be offensive to some people, as **2 Corinthians 2:15-16** clearly tells us: "For we are the aroma of Christ to God among those who are being saved and among those who are perishing, to one a fragrance from death to death, to the other a fragrance from life to life." Is it any wonder the world reacts so strongly toward Christians? To unbelievers, on some spiritual level they are not even aware of, we are the scent of death to them! This should give us compassion for unbelievers, but it should not make us compromise the Word of God or accept and tolerate things that are against the Bible. We need to speak out in the general sense, but be careful not to condemn or judge the individual sinner—a difficult balance to be sure, and one we can never pull off without the Holy Spirit!

There will definitely be things you will get push back on. People may ask, "How can God say He loves me when my life is such a mess?" "How could God allow this tragedy?" These are hard questions, for sure, and deserving of an answer. This is why giving the true Gospel message is crucial. In all of the parts of the Gospel message we have looked at, never did Jesus promise life would be easy or that we wouldn't have devastation in our life on Earth. While our difficulties are often the result of our own sin or the sin of someone else, sometimes, they are, sadly, the result of living in a broken world.

What we can find comfort in is that nobody understands pain and loss more than Jesus, yet He paid it willingly so that we could be with Him for all eternity. And unlike Jesus, Who faced His trials on His own, He promises that when we are His, He will be with us every step of the way and that none of our suffering will be in vain. And while knowing these things will not make the pain hurt any less, it may be what gives us the strength to keep going. It will turn "Why me, Lord?" into "How will you use this, Lord?"

The comfort of the Gospel is what Jesus has done for you. When we set our minds on that—appreciating, rejoicing, and resting in that—we will find strength we never knew we had.

Horatio Spafford understood what resting in the Gospel meant. That is why even after suffering the devastating loss of his four daughters, he was able to pen this hymn:

> *When peace, like a river, attendeth my way,*
> *When sorrows like sea billows roll;*
> *Whatever my lot, Thou hast taught me to say,*
> *It is well, it is well with my soul.*[36]

A final note on answering some of the hard questions we may be asked when presenting the Gospel: it is okay and completely appropriate to say that there are things we just cannot understand. Share what you know about Jesus and what He has done, and give yourself the freedom to admit there are things you do not know. You will find people will appreciate the honesty and humility.

---

36 Horatio G. Spafford, "It Is Well With My Soul," Public Domain, 1873.

Chapter 10
COUNTING THE COST

There is a difference between responsibility and cost. Responsibility is that which we are called to do. Cost is that which we are called to pay. Everything we do comes with a cost. Sometimes, the cost of something is very little; and sometimes, it can be great. Some costs we carefully consider before forging ahead, while others we may not even give a thought to. For example, I bet you have not spent a lot of time thinking about the cost of making dinner for your family: money to buy the food, time to prepare the food, frustration from someone inevitably whining, "I don't like this." In contrast, you probably put a great deal of thought into the cost when you purchased a home: the down-payment, the monthly mortgage payments, home owner's insurance, property taxes, the location, the school district, the neighbors, etc. When you became a Christian, did you think about the cost of following Jesus? If your answer is no, don't worry. You are not alone. In this chapter, we are going to look at that cost!

FOLLOWING *HIM* / *FOLLOWING* HIM

I once heard a pastor say, "Nobody ever stopped following Jesus because it wasn't worth it. They stopped because it was too hard." When we meditate on what Jesus has done for us, it makes our hearts melt, and it should! However, we should also spend time examining what the cost of following Jesus is.

In **Luke 14:28-30**, Jesus talks about weighing the cost of being His disciple. He compares it to a building project. "For which of you, desiring to build a tower, does not first sit down and count the cost, whether he has enough to complete it? Otherwise, when he has laid a foundation and is not able to finish, all who see it begin to mock him, saying, 'This man began to build and was not able to finish.'" In other words, Jesus is saying if you are going to start following Me, make sure you are prepared to go all the way. Bishop J.C. Ryle once said, "Nothing causes so much backsliding as enlisting disciples without letting them know what they are taking in hand."[37] So, what are we taking in hand when we become disciples of Jesus?

Jesus Himself answers that question in **Luke 9:57-62**:

> As they were going along the road, someone said to him [Jesus], "I will follow you wherever you go." And Jesus said to him, "Foxes have holes, and birds of the air have nests, but the Son of Man has nowhere to lay his head." To another he said, "Follow me." But he said, "Lord, let me first go and bury my father." And Jesus said to him, "Leave the dead to bury their own dead. But as for you, go and proclaim the kingdom of God." Yet another said, "I will follow you, Lord, but let me first say farewell to those at my home." Jesus said to him, "No one who puts his hand to the plow and looks back is fit for the kingdom of God."

This passage in Luke takes place at the end of Jesus' earthly ministry as He resolutely sets out for Jerusalem, knowing He will be crucified and killed there. On the way, He goes through Samaria, but was not welcome there because they found out He was going to Jerusalem. The Jews and the Samaritans were enemies. When the nation of Israel split, the Northern Kingdom of Israel had Samaria as its capital, while Jerusalem was the capital of the Southern Kingdom of Judah. The people of the Northern Kingdom intermarried with Assyrians and other foreigners and became a mixed-race

---

37 J.C. Ryle, *Expository, Thoughts on the Gospels With the Text Complete*, Ipswich: W. Hunt, 1856.

people, called Samaritans. When the people of Judah returned to the Promised Land to rebuild it, the Samaritans tried to undermine them. The Judahites called the Samaritans half-breeds and dogs and thought they were detestable. So not only was Jesus walking into His own death in Jerusalem, but on the way, He was rejected in Samaria by those who hated Him because of His lineage.

There are two things going on in this passage. For those who follow *Him*, there is the perfect, beautiful Person of Jesus. Nothing could be sweeter. However, in order to follow *Him*, we must also be willing to *follow* Him. *Following* Jesus means taking His path and being willing to risk enduring the same things He had to: rejection (like in Samaria), persecution, and death (like in Jerusalem).

In this passage from Luke, there are a total of three men contemplating following Jesus (v. 57, 59, 61). The incidents of each of the men is slightly different but serve to give a full picture of what *following* Jesus looks like for us. The first man comes to Jesus and says, "I'm ready to follow you; let's do this!" "And Jesus said to him, 'Foxes have holes, and birds of the air have nests, but the Son of Man has nowhere to lay His head'" (**v. 58**). Christ, the Son of God and the Messiah, is homeless! Jesus is telling the man that one of the costs of *following* Him is that you may have to forsake your material possessions—home, money, etc.

The second man doesn't jump to volunteer like the first. Instead, Jesus tells him, "Follow me" (**v. 59**). He is a little hesitant and says, "Lord, let me first go and bury my father." Jesus' answer—"Leave the dead to bury their own dead. But as for you, go and proclaim the kingdom of God" (**v. 60**)—may seem a little harsh; but we need to understand what is going on here. This man says he wants to follow Jesus, but just not right now. He has things he needs and wants to do first. This guy is saying, "I am comfy in this world right now; I'll follow you later." When we are saved, our sights should turn toward the things of God, not the things of the world.

The cost being laid out here is that to *follow* Jesus, you must be willing to turn your back on and stand against the things of this world—an action that can lead to rejection, hardship, and persecution. Jesus was on His way to Jerusalem to be beaten and killed. While this is all God's Sovereign plan, from an earthly perspective, it is brought about by the sinful actions of unbelievers because Jesus was not of the world and would not conform to it.

The third man says he wants to follow Jesus, but first wants to go back and say goodbye to his family. Jesus answers him, "No one who puts his hand to the plow and looks back is fit for the kingdom of God" (**v. 62**). Jesus' message is pretty blunt here. We need to put our hands on the plow and forge ahead in the service of God. The cost of *following* here? We must be all in! There is no place for a lukewarm Christian. We should be passionate about God and our faith. In gratitude for what Jesus has done for us, we should want to strive to serve and honor God in all that we do and say and in every area of our life. Logic dictates that the only way to possibly do this is to know about God. Therefore, we must do the work of studying God's Word and become grounded in Who He is and who we are to be.

These three accounts have one central message: to be a disciple (*follower*) of Jesus is costly. And while most of us will not lose our home or be killed for *following* Jesus, the point is, we must be *willing* to if needed. Jesus must be at the center and at the head of our lives. He must always be our top priority. Jesus is the Sustainer and Master of the universe. Everything belongs to Him! Yet He willingly, temporarily gave up His glory and His majesty to come to Earth as a Man and to save us. What He got in return were temptation, rejection, betrayal, heartache, torture, and death. If He was willing to pay all of that for us, is there any sacrifice that would be too great for us to pay for Him?

The first disciples of Jesus didn't think so. It wasn't just Jesus Who was born into a violent, cruel time in history under the Roman Empire; the first

Christians were living under this same sadistic regime. For some of the men and women who answered the call of Christ to *follow* Him, the ultimate cost was paid. Beginning with John the Baptist being beheaded by Herod and Stephen being stoned to death, the martyrdom of the early Christians was ongoing. From secular historians, we read how many of the early Christians were brutally tortured and killed. Every one of Jesus' apostles, except John, were executed. John was exiled to an island, but not before he was cast into a cauldron of boiling oil (miraculously, he was not injured). Here are a few examples of some guys you may recognize who met their death because they *followed* Jesus: James, John's brother, was beheaded; Philip was scourged and crucified; Matthew was impaled with a halberd (a spear/ax combo); James, Jesus' brother, was beaten, stoned, and thrown off of the temple roof; Matthias was stoned and beheaded; Mark, the writer of the Gospel of Mark, was dragged to pieces behind a horse; Peter was crucified upside down; Paul was beheaded; Jude, Bartholomew, and Andrew were crucified; Thomas was run through with a spear; and Luke, the writer of Luke and Acts, was hung from a tree.

Rather than be *discouraged* by the way the first disciples died, we should be *encouraged*! After Jesus' crucifixion, the apostles hid out, afraid for their lives. After the resurrection and receiving the Holy Spirit, these men went boldly out into the world preaching the Gospel, even when it meant dying a horrific death. Two important things we take away from this: One, they actually did see the resurrected Jesus (otherwise they would have never been willing to leave their hiding place); and two, it was only through the power of the Holy Spirit that they were able to be bold and brave.

Yes, *following* Jesus will be hard at times, but He never asks us to do it alone. The truth is, we never could do it alone. None of us are that strong on our own. It is only when we *follow* in the power of the Holy Spirit that we are able to forfeit our possessions, stand against this world, and be all in for Jesus.

FOLLOWING *HIM*

Sadly, persecution of Christians has continued throughout history right up until today. Right now, as you read this, Christians are being beaten, imprisoned, and killed just for their faith. North Korea still remains the most dangerous country in which to be a Christian; but Somalia, Afghanistan, Pakistan, Sudan, Syria, Iraq, Iran, and Yemen are close behind. In some of these countries, it is legal to kill Christians. For those who aren't killed, they are ostracized from society and left without any rights. They are unable to run a business, get a job, attend school, or socialize with neighbors. Yet these Christians willingly pay whatever price they have to in exchange for the joy and blessings they receive from following *Him*. Following *Jesus* is greater and more rewarding than anything we could ever imagine!

We receive forgiveness of sins, a relationship with Him, adoption into the family of God, the Holy Spirit living in us and sanctifying us, and living now and in eternal glory in the presence of God. Once we become Christians, we live *Coram Deo* (before God). **First Corinthians 2:9** says, "What no eye has seen, nor ear heard, nor the heart of man imagined, what God has prepared for those who love him." And **John 8:12** says, "Again Jesus spoke to them, saying, 'I am the light of the world. Whoever follows me will never walk in darkness, but will have the light of life.'"

These verses describe just a few of the many blessings we receive from following Jesus. May we, like so many before us, see that the costs of *following* Him could never outweigh the rewards of following *Him*.

Chapter 11

NO HALF-TRUTHS ALLOWED

Why is it so important that we get all of this right? The answer is because of what Jesus came to save us from. And what did He come to save us from? God. Yes, you read that correctly. Jesus came to save us from God. To be exact, He came to save us from God's wrath. Therefore, a false or half-truth Gospel message is not what you want to be believing yourself or sharing with others.

We're not trying to step on any toes here, although we may. What we are trying to do is to make you examine for yourself what you believe and what you are sharing with others. Christians are to examine and test themselves. They are literally to consider the question, "Am I really a Christian?" Paul tells the Corinthian church to do just that in **2 Corinthians 13:5**: "Examine yourselves, to see whether you are in the faith. Test yourselves. Or do you not realize this about yourselves, that Jesus Christ is in you?—unless indeed you fail to meet the test!"

We are not trying to say that you are not saved or that you've set out purposely to deceive others with a false gospel or half-truth (although there have been some who fall into that category). The truth is, it's easy to be deceived yourself if you don't know the truth. And if all you know is a false gospel, that is exactly what you will share with others.

JESUS, THE ONE AND ONLY WAY

In the closing verses of John nine, we see Jesus talking to the Pharisees, who are questioning Him after He healed the man who was born blind. This leads us into John 10, which is really a continuation of the conversation. In John 10:1-10, Jesus is talking to them about a sheep pen, the shepherds of the sheep, the Great Shepherd, and the door to the pen. The Church are the sheep; and they are exposed to deceivers, false prophets, and false teachers who come to steal, kill, and destroy. These imposters are the ones who climb over the wall to get into the sheep pen. They are not true shepherds; they are not true pastors. The true shepherds are those pastors who have received a true calling from God (which Jesus is telling the Pharisees they did not receive).

As for true shepherds, Jesus is also showing Himself as *THE* true Shepherd. But more importantly for this lesson, Jesus is also explaining here that He is *the* Gate. Jesus is the only true Way into the pen with the rest of the fold. In **John 10:11-13**, Jesus says, "I am the good shepherd. The good shepherd lays down his life for the sheep. He who is a hired hand and not a shepherd, who does not own the sheep, sees the wolf coming and leaves the sheep and flees, and the wolf snatches them and scatters them. He flees because he is a hired hand and cares nothing for the sheep."

The "hired hand" (the careless, neglectful pastor) will run when danger comes because he does not care for the sheep. In the church today, he will neglect his job of caring for the sheep, nurturing the sheep, and discipling the sheep. He is the pastor who will leave them with a shallow understanding of God and the Word. Likewise, he will not protect his flock from false teachings and false studies. Often, he will neglect his own study and growth in understanding the Bible.

In **John 10:14-18**, Jesus continues, telling them, "I am the good shepherd. I know my own and my own know me, just as the Father knows me and I know the Father; and I lay down my life for the sheep. I have other sheep that are not of this fold. I must bring them also, and they will listen to my voice. So there will be one flock, one shepherd." He continues His discussion with the Pharisees, saying that:

1. He lays down His life for the sheep, stating plainly that He laid it down of His own accord;

2. The Father loves Him because He will lay His life down and take it up again;

3. He has authority to lay it down and authority to take it up again—authority that was given to Him by the Father. No one else can take Jesus' life away from Him. He has full authority over His life.

In **John 10:27**, He tells us, "My sheep hear my voice, and I know them, and they follow me." In **John 14:6**, Jesus says, "I am the way, and the truth, and the life. No one comes to the Father except through me." **Matthew 11:27** says, "All things have been handed over to me by my Father, and no one knows the Son except the Father, and no one knows the Father except the Son and anyone to whom the Son chooses to reveal Him."

Peter, speaking to the Sanhedrin (the supreme council of the Jews headed by the high priest), tells us in **Acts 4:12**, "And there is salvation in no one else, for there is no other name under heaven given among men by which we must be saved." In **Romans 5:1-2**, Paul tells us why we have peace with God: "Therefore, since we have been justified by faith, we have peace with God through our Lord Jesus Christ. Through him we have also obtained access by faith into this grace in which we stand, and we rejoice in hope of the glory of God." Jesus is the Gate—the only Gate. Salvation is found in Him and in no other way. No other religion leads to God. No other paths lead to God.

WOLVES IN SHEEP'S CLOTHING AND AN ANTI-DECEPTION SELF-EXAMINATION

"Enter through the narrow gate. For wide is the gate and broad and easy to travel is the path that leads the way to destruction and eternal loss, and there are many who enter through it. But small is the gate and narrow and difficult to travel is the path that leads the way to [everlasting] life, and there are few who find it" (**Matt. 7:13-14 AMP**). This verse comes toward the end of Jesus' Sermon on the Mount. What is Jesus talking about here?

Some believe He was talking about the "gates" being entered at the end of life (since a gate at a residence is usually right before you enter the home). However, that is not what most commentators believe is true based on how the rest of the text is laid out. In the Sermon on the Mount, Jesus is talking to professing Christians about Kingdom life—what life in God's Kingdom will be lived like eventually and how we should strive to live this way as Christians now.

Similar to what we said about following *Him* or *following* Him in the previous chapter, Jesus is telling His followers that the path you follow as a Christian will be "through the narrow gate." In other words, the path you're going to follow is not going to be easy. On the narrow path, we will be expected to cooperate with the Holy Spirit to triumph over our natural inclinations—the sinful inclinations of our old nature at war with the new nature we've been given. Those sinful inclinations still cling to us because of our fallen sinful nature. Cooperating with the Holy Spirit to mortify them will feel like walking a very narrow road sometimes.

People on the broad path are dead in their sins. Either they have not yet had their hearts regenerated, or they never will. These people are lord of their own lives. This is why it is seemingly the easier path. What is easier than just calling your own shots about your life? It leads to destruction because people on this path are slaves to their sin nature.

So why would Jesus be telling professing Christians about the broad path at all? Wouldn't they already be on the narrow path? The next verse,

Matthew 7:15, tells us why: "Beware of false prophets, who come to you in sheep's clothing but inwardly are ravenous wolves." Why warn us here against false teachers? Because like we said before, Christians are to examine themselves. There are many people who believe they are Christians because they've been fed a false gospel—one that is centered on them, their hopes, and their dreams, with promises that God will fulfill them all. The warning about the gate being narrow, as well as Jesus' warnings from the book of John about false teachers, pastors, and false shepherds, should make you examine yourself and what kind of teaching you are believing.

How will you know a teacher is false? By knowing what the Bible says for yourself through careful study. However, if you haven't been steeped in careful study of the Scriptures, there is a way to spot a false teacher as we are told in the next few verses of Matthew 7. You will know them by their fruit!

> You will recognize them by their fruits. Are grapes gathered from thornbushes, or figs from thistles? So, every healthy tree bears good fruit, but the diseased tree bears bad fruit. A healthy tree cannot bear bad fruit, nor can a diseased tree bear good fruit. Every tree that does not bear good fruit is cut down and thrown into the fire. Thus you will recognize them by their fruits (**Matt. 7:16-20**).

You're probably sitting under a false shepherd or false teacher if you're hearing that God wants you to succeed, be happy, be rich, etc.; if the majority of your teaching comes from people who are focused on encouraging, supporting, and affirming you without often rebuking you; if your Christianity is based on God fulfilling your plans and your purposes; or if it's focused on what you can get from God and not on the glory and majesty of Christ and what He has done for you! In a very short summation of this, if the teaching you are getting from a Bible study, pastor, devotional, or conference is focused on *you*, you need to RUN AWAY as fast as possible!

These warnings are in the Bible for a purpose. False prophets and teachers have been around for a long time. The Israelites were fooled by them, and many Christians are today, also. Why is it so easy to fall prey to these people?

Because they tell us what our itching ears want to hear! It is very possible to think you are a Christian, do a lot of good works, serve in the church, and do all the things one thinks a Christian should do, only to find out at the end of your life that you are not one. Jesus said:

> "Not everyone who says to me, 'Lord, Lord,' will enter the kingdom of heaven, but the one who does the will of my Father who is in heaven. On that day many will say to me 'Lord, Lord, did we not prophesy in your name, and cast out demons in your name, and do many mighty works in your name?' And then will I declare to them 'I never knew you; depart from me, you workers of lawlessness" (**Matt. 7:21-23**).

Examine yourself. Examine your own fruit. Are you relying on the Gospel that teaches Christ died for your sins to save you from God's wrath? Have you seen changes in your lifestyle? Conviction of sin followed by repentance? Brokenness that leads to repentance whenever you've violated God's holy standards? Or are you relying on a gospel that makes you feel good? One that lets you live how you want without any conviction at all? One that tells you your problems are the result of something (or someone) else, other than your own sin? If so, you may be getting no real gospel at all. If the teaching you are getting sounds like the world's humanistic, self-help psychology, and the lifestyle you're living is like the world's, and you don't feel the Holy Spirit prompting you to repent, you might be on the broad path and not the narrow one!

Today, there are a good amount of "substitute gospels" being spread from many who claim to be evangelical Christians (some who may really believe that they are). Some of it is blatant; some is subtle. Human beings want to think that we are basically good, except for a few mistakes. We want to think God is waiting for us to decide what we want to do with our lives, and then He will bless it (if we're good enough). We want to think helping the poor or mission work is our ticket to Heaven. We want to substitute real Bible study with self-help books and co-commiseration with our peers about the bad things in our lives. We want our ministries to focus on relationships and fellowship, but without discipleship or the Gospel included in it.

And when it comes to spreading the Gospel, we want to tell people our own stories and the changes that happened in our lives when we became believers, without telling them the Gospel. We want to show them by our "actions." We want people to ask us what's different, instead of us telling them. At times, it seems like we'll try anything, except for actually sharing the complete Gospel message with people.

But if we truly believe that Jesus' substitutionary death on the cross in our place is the only way to not be an enemy of God, then we have to be clear about what we believe ourselves and what we tell others. With that being said, let's take a look at some things being substituted for proclamation of the true, complete Gospel message.

HALF-TRUTHS BEING TAUGHT TODAY

(WHAT IS NOT THE GOSPEL?)

Declaring that "Jesus is Lord" is true, but it is not the Gospel. That early confession is the only inspired, infallible, or inerrant confession passed down to us by the early Church, but it is not the Gospel! In **Romans 10:9**, Paul tells us, "Because, if you confess with your mouth that Jesus is Lord and believe in your heart that God raised him from the dead, you will be saved." Is that really all you have to do to be saved? Satan and his demons knew who Jesus was. They confessed it, as we see in **Luke 4:34**: "I know who you are—the Holy One of God." They also declare, "You are the Son of God" (**Luke 4:41**). And they ask, "What have you to do you with me, Jesus, Son of the Most High God" (**Luke 8:28**). Satan and his demons had no doubts about Who Jesus was. He is the Son of the Most High God. Therefore, He is Lord of all. Based on these verses, we can see that claiming Jesus is Lord is not enough.

These are good examples of why with all Scripture, context is of critical importance if we are to properly understand. Some churches are taking these verses out of context; and although there's truth there, it's not a saving truth! That is what so often goes wrong when we put too much emphasis on individual verses all by themselves. We need to use Scripture to interpret Scripture. That is how we get a true and correct understanding of the Bible.

So, let's take a look at what another Scripture passage says, where Jesus is declared "Lord" from **Acts 2:22-36**. Here we see Peter talking to the Jews who were questioning what was happening to the believers at Pentecost. Peter tells them these things:

1. That God showed them Jesus doing miracles in front of them (v. 22);

2. That Jesus was delivered up according to God's determined plan, using them to nail Him to a cross (v. 23);

3. That Jesus was raised from the dead (v. 24);

4. That it was Jesus Who fulfilled the Old Testament prophecy of David (v. 25-35);

5. That Jesus is both Lord and Messiah (v. 36).

Peter does not leave out the fact that Jesus is the Messiah, and neither should we! It is important that people understand Jesus is the Messiah, as well as being Lord. In the words of Kevin DeYoung from a sermon in October, 2012:

> Jesus is Lord. And if he's Lord over all, it means Jesus is my Lord. That's what you're saying when you confess Jesus as Lord. You're saying, "Jesus can call the shots for my life. Jesus can tell me how I should think about myself and about marriage and about the world. Jesus is the one who has all authority in heaven and on earth. Not me. I am not an autonomous creature. I live to serve this Master." That's what you're saying.[38]

Remember from chapter one when we said that God has the right to tell us how to live and also has the right to judge us because He is our Creator? That is why Peter is telling the Jews in Acts 2 that Jesus is not just Lord, but

---

38 Kevin DeYoung, "When We Confess Jesus As Lord," The Gospel Coalition, accessed October 18, 2018, https://www.thegospelcoalition.org/blogs/kevin-deyoung/when-we-confess-jesus-as-lord/.

that He is Messiah—their Savior! Peter tells them the whole truth because that is the Good News! He does not leave them with a half-truth, and we shouldn't leave people with one either!

"JUST ASK JESUS INTO YOUR HEART" IS NOT THE GOSPEL

Did you know that this phrase is not anywhere in the Bible at all? If you've been relying on the fact that you "asked Jesus into your heart" at some point, you may want to examine yourself. Likewise, promoting this as the idea of *how* to be saved is not a way of sharing the Gospel with someone. Paul Washer says this about it: "The greatest heresy in the American, Evangelical, and Protestant church is that if you pray and ask Jesus Christ to come into your heart, that He will definitely come in."[39]

Telling people to ask Jesus into their heart is not the Gospel. Some similar one-liners are:

- "Just pray this prayer, and you will be saved." You have to explain the Gospel.

- "Confess your sins." Catholic priests hear confessions every day. You have to explain the Gospel.

- "Give your heart to Jesus." This one can be very confusing, especially to a child! You have to explain the Gospel.

- "Invite Christ into your life." So, will He be living in the house with them now? You have to explain the Gospel.

There are more one-liners, but enough said. You have to explain the Gospel.

---

39 Paul Washer, "Shocking Youth message," accessed October 18, 2018, http://www.heartcrymissionary.com/sermons.

GETTING PEOPLE "FIRE INSURANCE" IS NOT THE GOSPEL

Some churches and some pastors focus on "getting people saved," usually with an eye toward having people come forth at an altar call, raise their hands saying that they recited the "Sinner's Prayer," or something similar. While the Gospel should be clearly put forth to people, if the focus of a worship service is on the "one-time 'getting saved' event" of a person's life, without any discipleship or teaching happening later, it's missing the point. The Gospel is not a product to be sold. Sinners are not consumers to whom you're trying to sell. Therefore, your message should not be a "commercial" for the Gospel. Instead of thinking of it that way, think of it as if you are a beggar showing other beggars where to get bread.

Becoming a Christian means a true heart change and a true life change—a life lived in repentance before God for the rest of the journey. This is not a one-time event that saves you from the fires of Hell after you die. If the Gospel message you were presented with or are presenting to others is only this type of "fire insurance" half-truth, then you may not actually be saved or be saving anyone else. Half-truths are not the Gospel.

YOUR TESTIMONY IS NOT THE GOSPEL

Testimonies are wonderful ways for the body of Christ to build one another up and are useful in many situations. While individual testimonies can lead to an explanation of the Gospel, many times (especially in support group type settings), the Gospel can get "sidelined" by personal stories of what Jesus has done in peoples' lives, with the explanation of sin and Christ's death to pay for it getting left out. Our conversion experiences should be used to back up our Gospel proclamation, not replace it. Jesus used Scripture to reveal Who He was, and we should, too! As Pastor Miles Rohde from Redemption Spokane Church puts it:

Most of our attempts at evangelism are often done by using personal life experiences—"I was like this, but because of Jesus, I am like this." Experiences are indeed important, but one of the most fundamental principles to remember in evangelism is that: **what you win people with, you will win them to.** Win them with experiences, and they will be won to experiences—devoted to move from one experience after another. And experiences DO NOT SAVE! Win them with promises of healing and material blessings or prosperity; you will win them to those things—equating health and wealth with salvation. And **absolutely NONE of those things SAVE!** Only JESUS Saves! Win people with Jesus and they will be won to Jesus![40]

In Acts, the apostles walk their hearers through the story of the Old Testament Scriptures, Christ's life, death, and resurrection. Stephen used Scripture in Acts seven; Paul and Silas used Scripture in Thessalonica; Philip uses Scripture to explain about Jesus in Acts 8; and the rest follow suit. They do not rely solely on their own testimony, stories, or experiences. None of those things would have taught the true Gospel message. As good as testimonies are, you have to go beyond that and present the whole Gospel message.

MERCY AND JUSTICE ARE NOT THE GOSPEL

Is the Gospel spread by the deeds of mercy and justice? Not only does the Bible say over and over that the Gospel is spread by preaching, but common sense tells us that loving deeds—as important as they are as an accompaniment of preaching—cannot, by themselves, bring people to a saving knowledge of Jesus Christ. Jesus' example was to take care of needs *and* explain the Gospel. As author and blogger Stephen Altrogge says:

---

40 Pastor Miles Rohde, "Sovereign Evangelism—ACTS: The Impact of Redemption," Sermon, accessed October 15, 2018, http://www.redemptionspokane.com/sermons.

> The people who say, "Preach the gospel, and use words if necessary," seem to forget that the very essence of the gospel is words. They might as well say, "Feed the poor, and use food if necessary," or, "Pay the bills, and use money if necessary." The gospel is primarily a message which must be communicated with words. It is good news which must be believed. The good news is that God sent Jesus to live and die in the place of sinners. People cannot embrace the good news if they don't first hear the good news. Feeding the poor is a good thing, but it isn't the same thing as proclaiming the message of the gospel. Caring for the homeless is a noble thing to do, but it isn't preaching the gospel. Preach the gospel, and use words, always.[41]

This should make us pause (as a Church) and ask ourselves: Are our church outreach programs and missions' activities about sharing the Gospel? Or are they just providing for needs (whether material or emotional), like the rest of the world is doing? If they are not outlets for verbally sharing the Gospel, are they conducive to instituting that into them, or should we do away with them altogether?

Yes, Christians are to do works of mercy and justice, but that by itself is not the Gospel. Need proof? Take a look at any disaster that happens in the world because "the world" is doing the same acts of service as we are. Mormons, Scientologists, humanists, and atheists are on the frontlines today reaching out to people, especially in disastrous situations. Only Christians will actually tell people the real Good News—that Jesus died in their place so that their sins could be forgiven and their relationship with God could be made right. Remember, *that* is a human's greatest need, so we need to make sure we tell them about it.

We have to make sure the Gospel is included, not because the "spiritual" is more important than the "physical," but because the "eternal" is more important than the "temporal."

---

[41] Stephen Altrogge, *The Inmates are Running the Asylum: Thoughts On Following Jesus, Amish Romance, the Daniel Plan, the Tebow Effect, and the Odds of Finding Your Soul Mate*, Kindle Edition. Indiana, PA: Blazing Center Books, 2014.

CHRISTIANS CARING FOR EACH OTHER IS IMPORTANT

One important thing to mention here, however, is that while serving the world in order to bring them the Gospel message is good, we also see examples in the Bible over and over again of Christians serving and taking care of each other. Paul actually states in **Galatians 6:10** that taking care of the people of God's household is first priority: "So then, as we have opportunity, let us do good to everyone, especially to those who are of the household of faith." God shows common grace toward all His creatures by doing good toward all, both the elect and the reprobate. He sends the rain on the just and the unjust. He feeds and clothes the pagan and the saint. He provides for the just and the unjust. But His saving grace is reserved for His own, for His Bride. We are to do good to all, like God does, but especially to the people of God, the household of faith.

By Christians caring for one another's needs, the world will see and know that Jesus was sent by the Father:

> "I do not ask for these only, but also for those who will believe in me through their word, that they may all be one, just as you, Father, are in me, and I in you, that they also may be in us, so that the world may believe that you have sent me. The glory that you have given me I have given to them, that they may be one even as we are one, I in them and you in me, that they may become perfectly one, so that the world may know that you sent me and loved them even as you loved me (**John 17:20-23**).

They will also see that we are His disciples by having love for one another. "A new commandment I give to you, that you love one another: just as I have loved you, you also are to love one another. By this all people will know that you are my disciples, if you have love for one another" (**John 13:34-35**). They will see the believers sharing with one another freely as told to us in **Acts 4:31-37**. Finally, they will see how believers handle strife when it arises between them and how they take care of the poor and widows as we see in **Acts 6:1-7**.

CREATING A MORE MORAL SOCIETY IS NOT THE GOSPEL

The Moral Majority of the 1970s and 80s and other evangelical Christian "civic advocacy" and political groups aimed at changing the culture through policy may have good effects on society and may be God-honoring in what they try to do, but it cannot be mistaken for the Gospel. "Redeeming the culture" is not the narrative of the biblical story. The main thrust of this idea is to change the world to be more "Christianized," reforming the culture through not only social justice and mercy, but also through government, the legal process, etc. to basically make the world and its people "good" by the time Jesus comes back. One way this is happening today is through the Religious Right, a political force moving behind and supporting conservative principals in government, all in an attempt to make a more moral society.

The problem is that moralism is not the point of the Gospel. While it's good for Christians to support godly laws, God-honoring politicians, and the like, we should reject completely the idea that the thrust of our "Kingdom work" means changing society along Christian lines. The goal of spreading the Gospel is to reach the elect by spreading it throughout the world so that they might hear it and believe. Laws never produce heart change, and morals—as good as they are—are not the Gospel.

"PARTNERING WITH GOD TO HELP BRING THE KINGDOM TO EARTH" IS NOT THE GOSPEL

Similar to and sometimes tied in with mercy and justice is an emphasis on helping God bring about the new heavens and the new earth. Some evangelicals are putting the primary emphasis of what they do onto God's promise to renew the world. In order to do this, they skip over the true Gospel message sinners need to hear about Jesus dying on the cross to save us from God's wrath. So many so-called evangelical preachers are skimming over the cross to make people feel happy! No one likes to hear that they are a sinner, but everyone likes the idea of a renewed world!

One example of this comes from a worldwide, very well-known relief organization that calls itself "Christian." And this organization serves the practical needs of many people around the world. However, absolutely nowhere on any of its websites does it proclaim that people are sinners separated from God and that they need to believe in Jesus' death on the cross as payment for it. This is just a small portion of what was on the website(s). Everything this organization states that it does is service-oriented to poor people all around the world. It is all aimed toward people "partnering with God" to bring about consummation of His kingdom. Here's an excerpt:

> The work of . . . in conjunction with the broader . . . is to alleviate poverty and to fight against injustice and oppression in all its forms. Our motivation for doing this runs deeper than a humanitarian response, important though that is. Our motivation is rooted in our desire to work in partnership with God to renew the world that God created. This work of renewal is manifested in our actions of development, relief and advocacy—work that we see as participating in bringing the kingdom of God on earth as it is in heaven" [abridged].

Jesus is saying that he is the embodiment of this good news. Through the life, death and resurrection of Jesus, sin and all that it entails has been done away with. This points to the holistic nature of salvation. As Tim C. explains, "Sin is the reign of evil and salvation is the overcoming of evil. Sin is expressed in hunger, injustice, sickness and spiritual alienation—in short, all that cripples the image of God. Salvation is expressed in food and justice, health and abundance that heals this crippled image. The good news is that we are called by God to partner with him to set things right." Jesus referred to this salvation as the kingdom of God.[42]

Food, justice, health, and abundance are all good things, but they're not the deepest need. And taking care of our fellow man's earthly needs (while it's a very good thing to do and Christians should be doing it) is not what will bring the Kingdom of God to Earth.

Often coupled with "remaking the world" and "promoting justice" are the issues of environmentalism and animal rights. In **Romans 8:22-23**, Paul tells us, "For we know that the whole creation has been groaning together in the pains of childbirth until now. And not only the creation, but we ourselves, who have the firstfruits of the Spirit, groan inwardly as we wait eagerly for adoption as sons, the redemption of our bodies."

It is true that some Christians wrongly have taken the idea that "subduing the world" gives them license to take and do anything they want to the environment and the creatures in it. The paradigm God sets for how we should treat animals and how we should feel about all of His creation is anything but how these Christians have acted.

However, other Christians have taken up environmentalism and animal rights as their Christian service to God. The extent to how big a role in our lives this should be is of big debate in the Church, often becoming political. It is an important discussion to have, but our first focus is proclaiming the Gospel.

The bottom line is, if we emphasize that God is remaking or renewing the world but do not include how He is redeeming people to be in it, we have not proclaimed the Good News to them. We have left them ignorant of the saving message of Jesus' death and resurrection. We do not partner with God to help bring the Kingdom to Earth, and remaking and renewing the world is not the Gospel.

---

42 "World Vision Australia—Our Christian Identity," accessed October 18, 2018, https://www.worldvision.com.au/docs/default-source/our-christian-identity/wva_oci_working_with_god.pdf?sfvrsn=2.

WHY IS THIS HAPPENING, AND WHAT CAN WE DO ABOUT IT?

Why does the Church, the Bride of Christ, want to shove sin, and death, and the glorious message of the cross out of our vocabulary? Is it because the ungodly don't like the message because we are an aroma that brings death to them as it says in **2 Corinthians 2:15-16**: "For we are the aroma of Christ to God among those who are being saved and among those who are perishing, to one a fragrance from death to death; to the other a fragrance from life to life. Who is sufficient for these things?"

Have we tried to become too relevant? Are people so self-centered that even the Church has to make their focus all about people and no longer about God? Is it because our good deeds make us feel good about ourselves, but we find it hard to bring up the Gospel to someone? Are we believing some of these half-truths ourselves? Are we more intent on what God can do for us than we are about studying His Word? Is it because we just don't know any better? Christian, it's time for that examination, and we start with the question to ourselves, "Am I really a Christian?"

If you are a Christian, as we've described over and over again in this book, then the next questions should be, "Am I sharing the whole Gospel message?" "Is my church sharing the whole Gospel message?" If not, then what do we do about it?

First of all, we make sure that we understand it. For our church, we make sure our church's members and attendees understand the whole Gospel message. We don't let them believe half-truths. We fight half-truths and the use of them. We make it our aim to see that people are taught the Bible well, that they have a clear and true understanding of the Bible's whole narrative, and then we proceed to learn more and more about Scripture through study. This is more than memorization of individual verses. It is learning to understand the Bible as a whole—both the Old and New Testament.

Let's make it our aim to glorify God by taking the message of the cross and making it central to everything else. "For the word of the cross is folly to those who are perishing, but to us who are being saved it is the power of God" (**1 Cor. 1:18**).

CONCLUSION

Whew! We know that was a lot! Obviously, we have gone through way more than you will probably ever tell someone when witnessing the Gospel. It may have been easier to just give the complete Gospel message to you in a few sentences. However, it's important to know the why and how and not just the what. The deeper your understanding of Scripture is, the clearer, and perhaps simpler, you will be able to articulate its truths to others.

Let's wrap up all that we have looked at:

- God, our holy, almighty Father has created us and everything else. As our Creator and Master, He has given us precepts on how we are to live.

- Because of Adam and Eve's rebellion against God, every person who has ever lived since has been born with a sin nature. As a result, everyone has broken God's precepts and sinned against Him. This makes us His enemies and deserving of His wrath and punishment of death and eternal damnation in hell.

- Before the foundation of the world, God, in His gracious mercy, chose a people to save and reconcile to Himself through His Son, Jesus Christ.

- Jesus, Who has always been, is, and always will be fully God, voluntarily left Heaven, temporarily forsaking His glory, to become fully Man. He chose to experience humanity exactly as we do. Unlike us, though, He lived a perfect life, which made Him an acceptable sacrifice to pay our debt with God and take our punishment. Because He was still fully God while He was fully Man, He was resurrected on the third day, an act that defeated Satan, sin, and death for His people once and for all.

- With the help of the Holy Spirit, our response to what Jesus has done needs to be to have faith (trust) in Jesus reconciling us with God and giving us forgiveness for our past, present, and future sins. This faith is *the only thing* we have to stand on before God.

- As a result of our new status before God, we are freed from the bondage sin once had on us. We shed our old selves by repenting of the sin in our life and cooperating with the Holy Spirit to become more and more like Jesus, a process that will not be completed until our mortal death or Jesus' second coming.

- Proof of our sanctification will be seen in the fruits we produce (how we live our life, how we serve God and others, and how our life has been transformed).

We invite you now to write down how you would present the Gospel message to someone and compare it to what you wrote back in chapter one. We encourage you to memorize it so that even when you have to tailor your delivery to your audience, your core message will always be the same.

Our prayer for you is that you have gained a deeper understanding of all of the elements of the Gospel message, that you feel impassioned to share this "too good to be true" news with all of those around you, and that God will bless you by using you to bring one of His elect to Him. Finally, we pray that you will be hungry for God's Word and that you will continue to keep digging into it and studying it. Just like quilt-making, the more you learn, the more you will realize you need to learn; but the more you will want to learn!

In Christ,

Chris & Rose

BIBLIOGRAPHY

"Albert Einstein - Everything Should Be Made as Simple as Possible, but No Simpler." Championing Science. https://championingscience.com/2013/11/10/everything-should-be-made-as-simple-as-possible-but-no-simpler (accessed October 12, 2018).

Altrogge, Stephen Altrogge. *The Inmates are Running the Asylum: Thoughts on Following Jesus, Amish Romance, the Daniel Plan, the Tebow Effect, and the Odds of Finding Your Soul Mate.* Indiana, PA: Blazing Center Books, 2014.

Bair, Bethany. "50 Questions to Ask Before Falling in Love." Lies Young Women Believe. http://www.liesyoungwomenbelieve.com/50-questions-ask-falling-love/?doing_wp_cron=1539359184.3302710056304931640625 (accessed October 12, 2018).

"Calvin's Commentaries." Christian Classics Ethereal Library. https://www.ccel.org/ccel/calvin/commentaries.i.html (accessed October 12, 2018).

"Chalcedonian Creed." Theopedia.com. https://www.theopedia.com/chalcedonian-creed (accessed October 15, 2018).

Darling, Daniel. "3 Ways Rising Secularism Affects Evangelism." The Gospel Coalition. https://www.thegospelcoalition.org/article/3-ways-rising-secularism-affects-evangelism (accessed October 12, 2018).

DeYoung, Kevin. "When We Confess Jesus As Lord." The Gospel Coalition. https://www.thegospelcoalition.org/blogs/kevin-deyoung/when-we-confess-jesus-as-lord/ (accessed October 18, 2018).

East, Kevin. "Building Sons Into Men" Crosswalk.com. https://www.crosswalk.com/blogs/kevin-east (accessed October 12, 2018).

Easton, M. G. *Illustrated Bible Dictionary.* New York: Cosimo Classics, 2005.

Fitzpatrick, Elyse. *Because He Loves Me: How Christ Transforms Our Daily Life.* Wheaton, IL: Crossway Books, 2008.

Jamieson, Robert, A.R. Fausset, and David Brown. "Bible Commentary Critical and Explanatory." Bible Study Tools. https://www.biblestudytools.com/commentaries/jamieson-fausset-brown (accessed October 18, 2018).

Kaiser, Walter C., Jr. "Jesus in the Old Testament." Gordon-Conwell Theological Seminary. https://www.gordonconwell.edu/resources/Jesus-in-the-Old-Testament.cfm (accessed October 15, 2018).

Kelly, Douglas F., Philip B. Rollinson, and Frederick T. Marsh. *The Westminster Shorter Catechism in Modern English.* Phillipsburg, NJ: Presbyterian and Reformed Pub., 1986.

"Luther at the Imperial Diet of Worms." Luther.de. https://www.luther.de/en/worms.html (accessed October 12, 2018).

Mathison, Keith. "Thy Kingdom Come by Keith Mathison." Ligonier Ministries. https://www.ligonier.org/learn/articles/thy-kingdom-come (accessed October 17, 2018).

Merriam-Webster. *s.v.* "Holy." https://www.merriam-webster.com/dictionary/holy (accessed December 12, 2018).

The New Strong's Exhaustive Concordance, Nashville, TN: Thomas Nelson Publishers, 1990.

"O.T. Names of God—Study Resources." BlueLetterBible.org. https://www.blueletterbible.org/study/misc/name_god.cfm (accessed October 18, 2018).

Packer, J. I. *Concise Theology: A Guide to Historic Christian Beliefs.* Wheaton, IL: Tyndale House Publishers, Inc., 1993.

Philip Schaff, ed. *The Nicene and Post-Nicene Fathers. First Series.* Vol. 108. Grand Rapids, MI: Eerdmans, 1979.

Piper, John. "What Is the Kingdom of God?" DesiringGod.org. https://www.desiringgod.org/interviews/what-is-the-kingdom-of-god (accessed October 17, 2018).

"Rick Warren Calls Pope 'Holy Father.'" Pulpit & Pen. https://pulpitandpen.org/2014/11/18/rick-warren-calls-pope-holy-father (accessed October 12, 2018).

Rohde, Pastor Miles Rohde. "Sovereign Evangelism – ACTS: The Impact of Redemption." Sermon, Redemption Spokane Church, Spokane, WA. July 17, 2016.

Ryle, J. C *Expository Thoughts on the Gospels.* Ipswich: W. Hunt, 1856.

"The Significance of Isaiah 53:4-5." Digital Image. Me.me. @poppafrank. https://me.me/i/the-significance-of-isaiah-53-4-5-ultimately-it-means-that-im-16236657 (accessed October 17, 2018).

Sproul, R. C. *The Holiness of God.* Carol Stream, IL: Tyndale House Publishers, 2006.

Spurgeon, Charles Haddon. *Sermons of Rev. C.H. Spurgeon of London.* S.I.: Forgotton Books, 2015.

Washer, Paul. "Shocking Youth Message." Sermon. July 27, 2002. Accessed October 18, 2018. http://www.heartcrymissionary.com/sermons-en#!sid=1.

"What's the Gospel?" Calvary Baptist Middletown.org. http://www.calvarybaptistmiddletown.org/cvglobal/?page=gospel&kw=gospel definition biblical&mt=b&loc=9007359&n=g&d=c&adp=2t1&c id=901509073&adgid=47684264289&tid=kwd-305745758046&gc lid=CjwKCAjwjIHeBRAnEiwAhYT2h4RMnQVLRWI2sUM7rl_ ZKQfwWNPNeBxHOYT58GUlPJ4wVjKOtrm0ehoCEskQAvD_BwE (accessed October 12, 2018).

Wikipedia. *s.v.* "Pelusium." https://en.wikipedia.org/wiki/Pelusium (accessed October 12, 2018).

"World Vision Australia—Our Christian Identity." Accessed October 18, 2018. https://www.worldvision.com.au/docs/default-source/our-christian-identity/wva_oci_working_with_god.pdf?sfvrsn=2.

For more information about
Christine Paxson and Rose Spiller
and
No Half-Truths Allowed
please connect at:

www.proverbs910ministries.com
www.facebook.com/prov910
proverbs910ministries@gmail.com
@prov_910

For more information about
AMBASSADOR INTERNATIONAL
please connect at:

www.ambassador-international.com
@AmbassadorIntl
www.facebook.com/AmbassadorIntl

If you enjoyed this book, please consider leaving us a review on Amazon, Goodreads, or our website.

Also check out Chris and Rose's Podcast: No Trash, Just Truth! *Streaming now on all platforms.*

More from Ambassador International

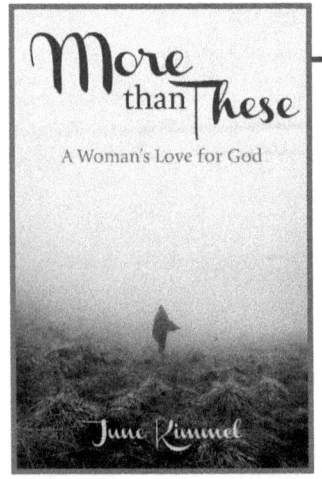

More Than These addresses the question that every woman who desires to walk with God must face: How can a woman love God as she should and keep the rest of her life in its proper place? Women are searching for the secret to balancing their lives. More Than These: A Woman's Love for God declares that loving God supremely is the answer.

More Than These
by June Kimmel

Could it be women are so busy chasing emptiness and playing the people-pleasing game, that they can't find time to live on mission? It's time to take a deep breath and do some inventory, to dig in and see what God's Word has to say about this tug-of-war between our flesh and our mission, and to figure out ways to quit chasing emptiness and take bold steps of obedience. What would happen if we said Enough of Me . . . more Jesus?

Enough of Me
by Priscilla Peters

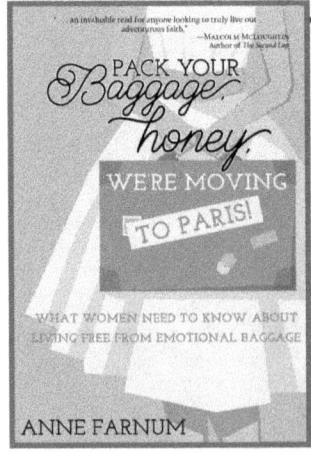

Using her own personal journey during an adventurous move to Paris, Anne shares healing truths of Scripture and methods she found to help others find freedom from their baggage. You will be inspired and refreshed as you realize you no longer have to carry your baggage either.

Pack Your Baggage, Honey, We're Moving to Paris!
by Anne Farnum

www.ingramcontent.com/pod-product-compliance
Lightning Source LLC
Chambersburg PA
CBHW070157100426
42743CB00013B/2945